CHURCH CHALLENGE

A multiple-choice trivia tour of church history

Marvin Hinten

BARBOUR
PUBLISHING, INC.
Uhrichsville, Ohio

CHURCH CHALLENGE

© MCMXCVIII by Marvin Hinten

ISBN 1-57748-369-3

Published by Barbour Publishing, Inc., P.O. Box 719, Uhrichsville, Ohio 44683 http://www.barbourbooks.com

Member of the
Evangelical Christian
Publishers Association

Printed in the United States of America.

SECTION 1

1. According to early church leader Tertullian (c. 200), why should men not shave?
   A. Shaving makes men too attractive to women
   B. If God had meant men to shave, they'd have been born with razor-sharp fingernails
   C. Men who shave are saying they can make themselves look better than God did
   D. Since women let their head hair grow long, men should let their chin hair grow long—it's only fair

2. *In His Steps* is the best-selling religious novel in history. To the nearest $10,000, how much money did publishers have to give author Charles Sheldon for it?
   A. $0
   B. $60,000
   C. $280,000
   D. $1,020,000

3. For what instrument was "Silent Night" originally written?
   A. Guitar
   B. Banjo
   C. Organ
   D. Piano

4. What was the comment of the man who invented individual communion cups in 1895?
   A. Hey, these are really cute!
   B. I'm tired of drinking other people's spit!
   C. Do they look too much like shot glasses?
   D. Now if only somebody would invent an easy way to fill these things

5. Who is Mrs. Amy Chapman?
   A. The first woman ordained in the United States
   B. A former atheist who converted to Christianity and wrote a bestseller about it
   C. The woman who started the rumor about Procter & Gamble's alleged Satanism
   D. A contemporary Christian singer

6. Who said, "If we had any possessions we should
   need weapons and laws to defend them. This
   would sometimes prevent us from loving God
   and our neighbors."?
   A. Justin Martyr
   B. William Law
   C. Pope Gregory I
   D. Francis of Assisi

7. In the hymn "There Is a Sea," what two seas are
   compared?
   A. Dead and Red
   B. Red and Black
   C. Black and Mediterranean
   D. Dead and Galilee

8. After Constantine became a Christian supporter,
   what did he have done to his wife and son?
   A. He had them murdered
   B. He had them baptized
   C. He divorced his wife and disin-
       herited his son because they wouldn't
       accept Christianity
   D. He had his son made a bishop and
       his wife made a deaconess

9. All of the following are lines from patriotic hymns. Which line belongs to our national anthem?
   A. "Then conquer we must"
   B. "And mercy more than life"
   C. "From war's alarms, from deadly pestilence"
   D. "Protect us by Thy might"

10. What type of church architecture became the most common shortly after A.D. 1000?
    A. Gothic
    B. Pyrrhic
    C. Romanesque
    D. Grotesque

11. John Wycliffe (1324–1384) translated the Bible into English. The government protected him during his lifetime; what did the church do forty-four years after his death?
    A. Dug up his bones, burned them, and threw the ashes into a river
    B. Killed his seven surviving grandchildren, twenty-six great-grandchildren, and six great-great-grandchildren
    C. Melted down his statue at Oxford
    D. Asked God to place him in "hell within hell"

12. Before Vatican II, in what language were Catholic worship services generally conducted?
    A. Greek
    B. Latin
    C. Hebrew
    D. English

13. Perhaps the two most famous religious mothers since Biblical times are the mothers of John Wesley and Augustine. What are their first names?
    A. Susanna and Monica
    B. Susanna and Gloria
    C. Juliana and Gloria
    D. Juliana and Monica

14. Why did many churches quietly drop the second verse of "Jesus Loves the Little Children" in the 1970s?
    A. It separates the Axis and Allied powers of World War II
    B. It doesn't say that Jesus loves American children
    C. It uses a term considered derogatory to the Japanese
    D. It conflicts with the Calvinist doctrine of limited atonement

15. In a 1983 survey, who was the most-watched TV preacher in America?
    A. Robert Schuller
    B. Jimmy Swaggart
    C. Jerry Falwell
    D. Oral Roberts

16. What alleged relic, kept in Canterbury, England, did the medieval church claim was the oldest relic in the world?
    A. The club with which Cain killed Abel
    B. The apple core from which Adam and Eve took bites
    C. A splinter of bone from Adam's rib
    D. The clay that God had left over after making Adam

17. How did religious hermit Simeon Stylites separate himself from the world the last twenty years of his life?
    A. He lived on the top of Mt. Olympus
    B. He lived on top of a fifty-foot pillar
    C. Although he could speak, he communicated only by sign language
    D. He let the rumor spread that he had leprosy, and people were afraid to get near him

18. In Italy in 1500, people were offered ten days off purgatory for each time they did what in church?
    A. Attended
    B. Took communion
    C. Stayed till the end of the service
    D. Stayed awake

19. What religious leader said the books that most influenced his life were the Bible and Leo Tolstoy's *The Kingdom Is Within You*?
    A. Tolstoy himself
    B. Billy Graham
    C. Jim Jones
    D. Mahatma Gandhi

20. Who said, "Within 100 years of my death, the Bible will be extinct"?
    A. Voltaire
    B. Napoleon
    C. Darwin
    D. Freud

21. In what country is the apostle Thomas traditionally supposed to have done his mission work?
    A. Spain
    B. England
    C. India
    D. China

22. What was the first religious book C. S. Lewis wrote, about which he said, "It was written before I knew how to write"?
    A. *Reflections on the Psalms*
    B. *The Pilgrim's Regress*
    C. *The Lion, the Witch, and the Wardrobe*
    D. *The Weight of Glory*

23. What is former president Carter's denominational affiliation?
    A. Anglican
    B. Baptist
    C. Catholic
    D. Methodist

24. Pope Urban II promised participants in the First Crusade all of the following except which?
    A. Freedom from tithing
    B. Guaranteed entry into heaven
    C. Reduced time in purgatory
    D. Exemption from taxes

25. Bob Tomato, Larry Cucumber, and Junior Asparagus are some of the starring characters in what Christian video series?
    A. Salad Days
    B. Fiber Fables
    C. Stew Stories
    D. Veggie Tales

26. What poet described Christ in "The Wreck of the Deutschland" as the "heaven-flung, heart-fleshed, maiden-furled Miracle-in-Mary-of-flame"?
    A. Matthew Arnold
    B. Dante Rossetti
    C. Algernon Swinburne
    D. Gerard Hopkins

27. Which of these hymns uses war imagery?
    A. "Rise Up, O Men of God"
    B. "Fling Out the Banner"
    C. "Lead on, O King Eternal"
    D. "Nearer, Still Nearer"

28. What Scripture does early church father Origen seem to have taken literally?
    A. Sell all that you have, and give it to the poor
    B. Some will become eunuchs for the kingdom of heaven's sake
    C. If a person strikes you on the right cheek, offer him your left
    D. They shall turn their spears into pruning hooks

29. Which of the following was not a common preparation for baptism in the second and third centuries?
    A. Fasting
    B. Being exorcised
    C. Being blessed
    D. Publicly breaking the ties of allegiance to one's parents

30. What famous short work begins, "Lord, make me an instrument of thy peace"?
    A. "The Prayer of the Confederate Soldier"
    B. "Footsteps"
    C. "The Touch of the Master's Hand"
    D. "The Prayer of Francis of Assisi"

31. What is the source of papyrus, the New Testament writing material?
    A. A plant
    B. An animal
    C. A mineral
    D. None of the above

32. Which of these hymns contains the name of a denomination in its first verse?
    A. "Jesus, Lover of My Soul"
    B. "And Can It Be?"
    C. "I Believe in a Hill Called Mount Calvary"
    D. "I Stand Amazed"

33. When George Whitefield toured America, he said bluntly, "The reason why congregations have been so dead is . . ."
    A. Because dead men preach to them
    B. Because they don't just quench the Holy Spirit, they hold His head under, out of sight
    C. Because they don't even know whether there is a Holy Spirit
    D. Because they stab each other's backs

34. There are more extant manuscripts of the Bible and the *Iliad* than of any other ancient works. How do their manuscript numbers compare?
    A. There are an almost identical number of manuscripts for each
    B. There are four times as many Bible manuscripts
    C. There are forty times as many Bible manuscripts
    D. There are 400 times as many Bible manuscripts

35. Identify this writer: "What a vast distance there is between knowing God and loving Him!"
    A. Blaise Pascal
    B. Barton W. Stone
    C. Felix Mendelssohn
    D. King James I

36. Which of these is not a well-known campus religious organization?
    A. Fellowship of Christian Athletes
    B. The Holiness Club
    C. Navigators
    D. Inter-Varsity

37. In the mid-1970s, how many Bibles and Scripture portions were the United Bible Societies distributing each year?
    A. 25,000
    B. 2,500,000
    C. 250,000,000
    D. 25,000,000,000

38. Which of the following was not a branch of trade opposed by nineteenth-century missionaries?
    A. Opium
    B. Slaves
    C. Alcohol
    D. Tobacco

39. What is the denominational affiliation of former president Richard Nixon?
    A. Quaker
    B. Seventh-Day Adventist
    C. Lutheran
    D. None

40. What is the religious importance of Transylvania?
    A. When the vampire scare hit here, church membership reached 100 percent, which has happened nowhere else
    B. Transylvania, Inc., is owned by Phillip Polchansky, the leading philanthropist in Baptist history
    C. Transylvania is a Disciples of Christ college in Kentucky
    D. Bram Stoker donated fifty percent of his royalties from *Dracula* to building cathedrals here

41. When Origen did his commentary on the Gospel of John, how much material did the first volume cover?
    A. Only the first six chapters
    B. Only the first chapter
    C. Only the first six verses
    D. Only the first six words

42. Which translation is not correctly matched with its publisher?
    A. New American Standard—Bethany
    B. New International—Zondervan
    C. New King James—Thomas Nelson
    D. Living—Tyndale House

43. If 1099 is a date rather than an IRS form, what is its significance?
    A. People thought it was the end of the millennium, so there was a widespread (but short-lived) revival
    B. The Crusaders took Jerusalem that year
    C. Astrologers predicted another Messiah would be born that year, which led to a church split
    D. Bonaventure was born, Francis of Assisi was converted, and Bernard died, all in the same year

44. What book of the Bible furnished the lyrics for the Byrds' hit song "Turn, Turn, Turn"?
    A. Psalms
    B. Proverbs
    C. Ecclesiastes
    D. Song of Solomon

45. The church at Rome in the fifth century divided its income four ways, with one-fourth going to the bishop. Which of the following did not receive a one-fourth share?
    A. Other clergymen
    B. Building maintenance
    C. Missions and evangelism
    D. The sick and poor

46. Early Christians were deeply concerned about the poor. According to Clement, what did some Christians of his day (c. A.D. 100) do to help the needy?
    A. Killed themselves and in their wills left everything to the poor
    B. Sold themselves into slavery and gave the purchase price to the poor
    C. Prayed for poor Christians to find gold pieces as they walked along roads
    D. Ate only on alternate days and gave the food from the other days to the poor

47. "Angels We Have Heard on High" was originally written as a macaroni carol. What does that literary term mean?
    A. It was written in Italian by a person for whom Italian was not his native language
    B. It was meant to be sung each year at the "Partazzi Pasta," or Feast of Macaroni
    C. The lyrics were written in two different languages, Latin and French
    D. It was intended to be sung staccato, as opposed to a spaghetti carol (flowing)

48. What country possesses the tallest church tower?
    A. Germany
    B. France
    C. The United States
    D. Romania

49. What Christian leader said, "We shall match your capacity to inflict suffering with our capacity to endure suffering"?
    A. Justin Martyr, about the Romans
    B. Felix Manz, about the Protestants
    C. Corrie ten Boom, about the Nazis
    D. Dr. Martin Luther King, Jr., about the white racists

50. In western Europe in the late fourth century, what portion of one's inheritance was traditionally left to the church at death?
    A. One-tenth
    B. One-fifth
    C. Everything, provided one's children were all over the age of twenty-one; otherwise, one-tenth
    D. The amount that would have been left to another child if the family had had one more birth

51. Martin and Katie Luther had several of his friends in their bedroom on their wedding day. Why?
    A. In Germany at that time, it was customary to have witnesses observe the marriage consummation
    B. Catholics had vowed to kill Martin and Katie before they could produce "schismatic offspring"

    C.   It was customary to "bless the bed" to make the wife more fruitful

    D.   Martin and Katie had no guest bedroom, so they had to keep friends who had come in for the wedding

52. What were the two key pieces of evidence used by second-century Christians to support their belief in Christianity?
    A.   Christ's miracles and fulfillment of prophecy
    B.   Christ's miracles and "internal witness"
    C.   "Internal witness" and fulfillment of prophecy
    D.   Fulfillment of prophecy and rapid church growth

53. What does transubstantiation mean?
    A.   People being allowed to transfer membership to a different congregation without examination or letter
    B.   Belief that Communion bread and wine smell and taste the same but become Christ's actual body and blood
    C.   Being able to prove one's point from both the New Testament and from nonbiblical sources
    D.   A promise in medieval times to atone for a heresy with a life of good works

54. In the standard tune of "The Lord's Prayer"
    (Malotte), which syllable requires the highest note?
    A. "Will"
    B. "Glo" in "glory"
    C. "Ev" in "ever"
    D. "A" in "amen"

55. Which of the following leaders involved in the
    scandals of the late 1980s voluntarily submitted
    to church discipline?
    A. Oral Roberts
    B. Gordon MacDonald
    C. Jim Bakker
    D. Jimmy Swaggart

56. An average of how many new churches were
    built per decade in eleventh-century France?
    A. None
    B. Twelve
    C. Forty-five
    D. 160

57. When Quaker founder George Fox wanted to be
    filled spiritually, he asked three Church of
    England ministers what to do. Which of these is
    not one of the answers he got?
    A. Sleep ten hours a night
    B. Smoke tobacco and sing psalms
    C. Get married
    D. Lose blood

58. To avoid persecution in A.D. 250, Christians had
    to possess a certificate saying that they had—
    A. Blasphemed Christ
    B. Sacrificed to idols
    C. Knelt before a statue of the emperor
    D. Not been baptized

59. Of the original thirteen colonies, how many had
    Protestant origins?
    A. Six
    B. Eight
    C. Ten
    D. Twelve

60. Of which organization is Bill Bright "founder
    and president"?
    A. Young Life
    B. Youth for Christ
    C. Campus Crusade for Christ
    D. Navigators

61. In the thirteenth century, most laypeople could
    not read, so what became known as "the scripture
    of the laity"?
    A. Religious artwork
    B. Preaching
    C. Lives of saints
    D. Dramas performed outside churches

62. Jonathan Edwards, author of "Sinners in the Hands of an Angry God," was pastor of a frontier church for seven years. Why did he spend almost all of his time there in his study?
    A. The people smelled like bear grease, an odor he couldn't tolerate
    B. The congregation included only three families besides his own, so it didn't require much pastoral care
    C. He was always sick; the year after he left it was found that raw sewage emptied into his drinking water
    D. After seeing Indian rituals, Edwards decided that the forest was Satan's, and he feared to leave his house

63. For several years in the fourteenth and fifteenth centuries there were two popes. When the Council of Pisa met in 1409 to resolve this situation, what happened?
    A. They had one of the popes killed on the grounds that it was expedient for one man to die for the church
    B. They asked God to decide, and nine days later one of the popes got a fever and died
    C. They deposed both popes, and the church was led by councils for the next forty years
    D. They selected a new pope, but the other two both excommunicated him, so the church wound up with three popes

64. Francis of Assisi started the Franciscans, but surprisingly, he was not a Franciscan when he died. What rule did the pope make that caused Francis to leave?
    A. That the members of the order could have mistresses
    B. That the order could own property
    C. That Franciscans could eat meat
    D. That the order's ultimate allegiance was no longer to Francis, but to the pope

65. According to Justin Martyr, in A.D. 150, was Communion taken to people who could not attend church?
    A. No, that wasn't considered necessary
    B. Only if they had no relatives to partake of it for them
    C. Yes, particularly if they were sick or in prison
    D. Yes, but only if they had not partaken in the past twenty-eight days

66. Junipero Serra founded more missions in America than any other explorer, despite a life-long thorn in the flesh from his first American journey. How did he get wounded?
    A. A chigger bite
    B. An Indian arrow
    C. A cactus needle
    D. A wolf bite

67. What are catechumens?
    A. Demons from Greek mythology that
       were half-cattle, half-human
    B. Christians who met in catacombs
    C. People undergoing instruction for
       baptism
    D. The candles used in the fifth century
       to examine a person's throat during
       an exorcism

68. Which of the following was Freud's description
    of religion?
    A. The ultimate crutch of the mentally
       lame
    B. The universal obsessional neurosis
       of humanity
    C. The dust jacket on the book of life—
       attractive, but irrelevant
    D. What the world needs now—it's
       the only thing that there's just too
       little of

69. A hymn parody about dispensationalists a few
    years back went, "My hope is built on nothing
    less/Than _____ notes and Moody Press."
    What Bible editor's name went in the blank?
    A. Lenski's
    B. Boettner's
    C. Keil's
    D. Scofield's

70. Where was Christian traveling to in *The Pilgrim's Progress*?
    A. Celestial City
    B. Heavenly Haven
    C. Visionary Village
    D. Blessedburg

71. Though many people wanted Spain united, the devout Isabella hesitated to marry Ferdinand because they were cousins. How was this scruple overcome?
    A. The pope wrote a letter saying that cousins could marry if doing so united a kingdom
    B. A Spanish archbishop forged the pope's signature to a letter saying they could marry
    C. She used Columbus's voyage as a "fleece"; she and Ferdinand did not consummate their vows until Columbus returned
    D. Ferdinand revealed to her that he was illegitimate, so technically they weren't cousins

72. Which of these colonies was most like contemporary America in its religious freedom and diversity?
    A. New Amsterdam
    B. Plymouth
    C. Massachusetts Bay
    D. Jamestown

73. According to a *Psychology Today* article, where did pastors place on the Duncan scale of job prestige for "respected and desirable professions"?
    A. Number 94, between dentists (95) and lawyers (93)
    B. Number 72, tied with teachers and retail store buyers
    C. Number 63, between insurance agents (66) and librarians (60)
    D. Number 52, between manufacturing foremen (53) and power station operators (50)

74. Blaise Pascal was history's greatest combination mathematician-religious writer. He did all of the following except which?
    A. Developed the theory of probability
    B. Proposed the four-color map problem
    C. Invented the adding machine
    D. Wrote the *Pensées*, a major seventeenth-century work of religious thought

75. What president wrote that he would like to see built "a wall of separation between church and state"?
    A. George Washington
    B. John Adams
    C. Thomas Jefferson
    D. Abraham Lincoln

76. Which of these cities is incorrectly matched with its claim to fame?
    A. Grand Rapids, Michigan—Christian publishing
    B. Independence, Missouri—Christian seminaries
    C. Nashville, Tennessee—Christian music
    D. Colorado Springs, Colorado—Christian organizations

77. Amidst all the fasting and other features of the fifth-century ascetics, perhaps the most exhausting ritual was performed by the "acoimetai." What did they do?
    A. They had to preach the gospel to a different tribe every day of the year
    B. They had to remain attached to an eighty-pound cross at all times
    C. They had to swim slightly over six miles a day to signify being "born of the water"
    D. They had to sing a praise song every three minutes round the clock, seven days a week

78. What religious term comes from a Latin root meaning "wonder"?
    A. Skeptic
    B. Agnostic
    C. Miracle
    D. Incarnation

79. The sixteenth-century Christian scholar Erasmus wrote a classic etiquette book that remained a bestseller for two hundred years. It contained all the following rules except which?
    A. If you can't swallow a piece of food, turn around and throw it somewhere
    B. Don't lick your fingers if they get greasy; what do you think a table-cloth is for?
    C. Do not spit onto your plate unless you're sure you are finished eating
    D. Do not keep your vomit in your mouth; let it come out where it belongs

80. Which of the following is not a line from the Pledge of Allegiance to the Christian flag?
    A. I pledge allegiance to the Christian flag
    B. And to the Savior for whose kingdom it stands
    C. One brotherhood, under God, uniting all Christians
    D. In service and in love

81. At the end of the nineteenth century in America, there was one Protestant church per how many citizens?
    A. 450
    B. 900
    C. 4,500
    D. 9,000

82. What was the Anabaptist analogy showing why
    they required a changed life before baptism
    rather than after?
    A. You can't tan a hide while it's still
       on the deer
    B. You can't wash a cabbage while it's
       down in the dirt
    C. You can't roller-skate in a buffalo
       herd
    D. You don't give away your merchan-
       dise until you see the buyer's money

83. When gospel singer Andrae Crouch was arrested
    for possession of cocaine in 1985, what did the
    white powder in his car turn out to be?
    A. Salt
    B. Sugar
    C. Instant chicken soup mix
    D. Cocaine, but such a small amount
       that the sentence was suspended

84. Which of these is not a religious claim to fame of
    the Siloam Springs, Arizona area?
    A. The country's largest Christian health
       spa
    B. A huge showplace of Precious
       Moments figures
    C. John Brown University
    D. The headquarters of a major
       Christian greeting card company

85. What was the official church title of multiple murderer Thomas de Torquemada?
    A. His Holiness, the Pope
    B. The Grand Inquisitor
    C. Doctor of the Church
    D. Official Church Murderer

86. According to a hymn, what is the only way "to be happy in Jesus"?
    A. To let His love seize us
    B. To trust that He'll please us
    C. Let Him heal our diseases
    D. Trust and obey

87. According to one source, why did John Wesley say he did not expect to see Methodist evangelist George Whitefield in heaven?
    A. "He'll be so close to God's throne, and I'll be so far away, I won't be able to see him!"
    B. "I'm planning to live in the big mansions marked 'Grace,' and he'll be staying in the little shacks marked 'Works'!"
    C. "Although Mr. Whitefield talks a good deal about the Lord, I am not sure they have ever been formally introduced"
    D. "Whitefield won't be able to stay in heaven. He'll be out preaching to the fallen angels!"

88. In *Future of an Illusion,* Sigmund Freud argued
    that the idea of a benevolent Creator is a classic
    case of what?
    A. Stupidity
    B. Wish-fulfillment
    C. Waking dreams
    D. Oedipus complex

89. Which of the following four Bible translations is
    considered the most literal?
    A. New American Standard
    B. New International
    C. Revised Standard
    D. New King James

90. What nature song is known as "The Crusaders'
    Hymn"?
    A. "For the Beauty of the Earth"
    B. "This Is My Father's World"
    C. "Fairest Lord Jesus"
    D. "How Great Thou Art"

91. What sort of creature is Bilbo Baggins?
    A. A hobbit
    B. A gnome
    C. A woozle
    D. A marshwiggle

92. What fifteenth-century leader had, ironically, been previously given the title "Defender of the Faith" by the pope?
    A. John Calvin
    B. Martin Luther
    C. Henry VIII
    D. Ulrich Zwingli

93. In Nathaniel Hawthorne's *The Scarlet Letter,* what was the letter and what did it stand for?
    A. A for Adultery
    B. H for Harlot
    C. H for Heretic
    D. P for Prostitute

94. What sixteenth-century New Testament religious movement was known for these principles: separation of church and state, believers' baptism, immersion, and pacifism?
    A. Wycliffites
    B. Anabaptists
    C. Savanarolans
    D. Children of Light

95. What is the Turkish word for "lion"?
    A. Leo
    B. Simba
    C. Melchior
    D. Aslan

96. What hymn was appropriately written by a man who died the same evening he wrote it, clutching the words in his hand?
    A. "Beyond the Sunset"
    B. "Lord, I'm Coming Home"
    C. "Abide with Me"
    D. "O Love, That Wilt Not Let Me Go"

97. Our word "noon" comes from Latin "nona," or ninth hour, which is 3:00 P.M. Why do we now have noon at 12:00 rather than 3:00?
    A. Benedictine monks were not allowed to eat until noon; if they called 12:00 noon, they could eat earlier
    B. Francis of Assisi felt we should not celebrate the middle of the day at the hour when Christ died
    C. The Jews had noon at 3:00, so second-century Christians changed it to distinguish themselves
    D. Augustine "proved" that God created the world at the darkest time, midnight, so that should start the day

98. In the pre-hymnal days, the song leader would say a line from a hymn, and then the congregation would sing it. What was this process called?
    A. Singing slowly
    B. Lining out
    C. Passing the word along
    D. Following the leader

99. How did Luther put up his Ninety-five Theses?
    A. With glue
    B. With a nail
    C. With tape
    D. With Plasti-tak, left over from the
        Wittenberg VBS

100. What knight of the Round Table obtained the
     Holy Grail "because his heart was pure"?
     A. Lancelot
     B. Galahad
     C. Percival
     D. Arthur

101. Which of Dr. Martin Luther King's works cen-
     ters on Christian apathy, as in "I have been so
     greatly disappointed with the white church and
     its leadership"?
     A. "Letter from Birmingham Jail"
     B. "I Have a Dream"
     C. "Stride toward Freedom"
     D. "Why We Can't Wait"

102. "My son, eat thou honey, because it is good."
     What translation of Proverbs 24:13a is this?
     A. New International
     B. Amplified
     C. Good News
     D. King James

103. In what century was celibacy first enforced upon the clergy?
    A. Third
    B. Seventh
    C. Eleventh
    D. Fifteenth

104. It is said that mothers hid their sons and wives hid their husbands when Bernard of Clairvaux came around. Why?
    A. Bernard was so persuasive in describing the joys of being a monk that hardly anyone could resist
    B. Despite his commitment to Christ, Bernard was a homosexual
    C. Bernard had the pope's authority to draft whomever he wanted for the Crusades
    D. Women in medieval times could ask spiritual questions in the presence of one man, but not more than one

105. In the sixteenth century, approximately what percentage of Russian land was owned by the church?
    A. One
    B. Five
    C. Ten
    D. Thirty

106. The first female pastor in America, Antoinette
     Brown, went to seminary from 1848–1850.
     Because she was female, how long was it before
     the seminary granted her degree?
     A. Seven years
     B. Fourteen years
     C. Twenty-one years
     D. Twenty-eight years

107. What does the Latin word *haeresis,* from which
     we get heresy, mean?
     A. Evil
     B. Choice
     C. Original
     D. Insane

108. Why are there early Christian prayers of bless-
     ings on olives?
     A. There had been a blight on olive
        trees and Christians were trying to
        "resurrect" the crop
     B. Poor people sometimes put olives
        in the offering instead of money
     C. There was a movement to consecrate
        olives to the emperor, which would
        violate Christian consciences
     D. Olives were an early Christian
        symbol; the oil stood for Christ's
        blood

109. What is simony?
    A. Naming a child after Simon Peter
    B. Caring more for waxing a car than for painting the church building
    C. Buying a church position
    D. Accepting general Catholic theology but not the headship of the pope

110. Michelangelo did a famous eighteen-foot-tall statue of what Biblical figure?
    A. Abraham
    B. Noah
    C. Saul
    D. David

SECTION 2

1. One of the most famous saints of the fifth century was Melania the Younger. At age twenty she decided to "renounce the world," including all these except which?
   A. Sexual relations with her husband
   B. Food except for once every five days
   C. Shelter from the rain or snow
   D. Her dependence on slavery (she freed 8,000 of her slaves)

2. "What are men better than sheep or goats. . . If, knowing God, they lift not hands of prayer/Both for themselves and for those who call them friend"? What work is this from?
   A. Dante's *Divine Comedy*
   B. Browning's *The Ring and the Book*
   C. Shakespeare's *Measure for Measure*
   D. Tennyson's *Idylls of the King*

3. What contemporary cross-cultural Bible translation equates Jews and Samaritans with whites and blacks?
   A. The Southern-Fried Version
   B. The Cotton Patch Version
   C. The Heart of Dixie Version
   D. The Peach Tree Version

4. By what name is the Church of Jesus Christ of Latter-Day Saints better known?
   A. Jehovah's Witnesses
   B. Moonies
   C. Christian Scientists
   D. Mormons

5. A fourth-century woman named Olympias was famous for her holiness and modesty. According to the fifth-century biography *Life of Olympias,* how modest was she?
   A. She kept her clothes on while bathing so that she wouldn't see herself naked
   B. After the age of fourteen she never looked at her own image again in a mirror or even in a pool of water
   C. When a visiting bishop preached to her convent, she wore her long hair forward, to hide her face
   D. After entering the convent she never initiated another conversation, but spoke only when spoken to

6. *Paradise Lost* is, as most people know, about the fall of Adam and Eve. But what is *Paradise Regained* about?
   A. Christ's birth
   B. Christ's temptations
   C. Christ's crucifixion
   D. Christ's resurrection

7. Which of these is a line from the "Prayer of the Confederate Soldier"?
   A. My child, those were the places where I carried you
   B. In the doing of my duty/ Let me never kill a brother
   C. I was given infirmity, that I might do better things
   D. For God, for love of country/ For friends and family

8. Joy Davidman and C. S. Lewis married each other twice. Why?
   A. They got a divorce from their first marriage to each other, then reconciled and remarried
   B. The first wedding was a civil ceremony; the second was done by a priest
   C. The first marriage was annulled because, due to Joy's cancer, it went more than a year without consummation
   D. The second time was not an actual marriage; they simply resaid their vows for their fifth anniversary

9. In medieval England, what was a "neck verse"?
   A. If a person committed a crime, he had to wear around his neck the Bible verse that condemned that crime
   B. It was a nickname for the stocks (labeled with the misdeed) where criminals against morality were put
   C. If a clergyman had committed a hanging crime, he could be spared by reading an assigned verse
   D. It was a brand of condemnation placed on heretics, later also forced on Jews

10. In A.D. 388 the Roman Emperor Theodosius ordered a Christian bishop to build a Jewish synagogue. Why?
   A. Theodosius had just converted from Christianity to Judaism and wanted a place to worship
   B. The bishop's church had burned down the previous synagogue
   C. In a unity move, Theodosius was having a leader from each religious group make a house of worship for others
   D. The Jews had rioted and torn down a church, and Theodosius did this as a way of turning the other cheek

11. Taking their cue from Psalm 119 ("Seven times a day will I praise Thee"), medieval monks prayed daily at three-hour intervals, starting at noon. What interval did they skip?
    A. 6:00 P.M.
    B. 9:00 P.M.
    C. Midnight
    D. 3:00 A.M.

12. What is the opposite of Calvinism?
    A. Arminianism
    B. Nestorianism
    C. Apollonarianism
    D. Antidisestablishmentarianism

13. "Jesus, the very thought of Thee/With sweetness fills my breast." But according to that hymn, what is even sweeter?
    A. Jesus' wounds
    B. Jesus' love
    C. Jesus' heart
    D. Jesus' face

14. Eighteenth-century Quaker businessman John Woolman thought long workdays led to drunkenness. What length of workday did he advocate?
    A. Six hours
    B. Eight hours
    C. Ten hours
    D. Twelve hours

15. If a seventeenth-century Baptist in England wanted to tithe to his church, he actually had to give up twenty percent of his money. Why?
    A. Since a tithe was ten percent to the Jews, Baptists reasoned Christians should be twice as grateful
    B. Baptists were required to give to missions an amount equal to what they gave to the local church
    C. To make people leave the Baptists (where most tithers were), Parliament passed a law defining "tithe" as twenty percent
    D. Everyone was required to give ten percent to the Anglican Church no matter what religion they supported

16. Susanna Wesley is often held up on Mother's Day as the ideal mother, but it appears she focused too much on her sons. All of these happened to her daughters except which?
    A. The oldest, Emilia, griped continually and her husband left her after a few years of marriage
    B. Susanna Jr. married a man her mother called "little inferior to the apostate angels in wickedness"
    C. Hetty ran off with a man who deserted her, and she married another man when she was four months pregnant
    D. Kezzy became an alcoholic, then an opium addict, and died at the age of thirty-two

17. All of the following are true of early twentieth-century Christian writer G. K. Chesterton except which?
    A. He became a Hindu in college and didn't return to Christianity till age twenty-nine
    B. He wrote mysteries featuring a priest, Father Brown, as the detective
    C. His *The Everlasting Man* was a major influence on the spiritual growth of C. S. Lewis
    D. He was one of the heaviest Christian writers of this century, at over 300 pounds

18. In Chaucer's *Canterbury Tales,* what martyr were the pilgrims making their journey to honor?
    A. Stephen
    B. Justin Martyr
    C. Thomas More
    D. Thomas à Becket

19. What World War I religious leader helped his listeners take a "Christian" view of their enemies by labeling them "pretzel-chewing sauerkraut spawn of bloodthirsty Huns"?
    A. Lyman Beecher
    B. William Jennings Bryan
    C. Will Graham (Billy's father)
    D. Billy Sunday

20. What letter did Martin Luther call "my epistle, to which I am betrothed"?
    A. Galatians
    B. Ephesians
    C. Philippians
    D. Colossians

21. What Christian children's series has been criticized for giving blacks lines like "I be gwine to put some liquid stuff dat you cain't see 'round de flo'. But it stink good"?
    A. The Mandie books
    B. The Dallas O'Neil books
    C. The Sugar Creek Gang books
    D. The Chronicles of Narnia

22. "Music makes people kinder, gentler, more staid and reasonable. The devil flees before the sound of music almost as much as before the Word of God." What musician said this?
    A. John W. Peterson
    B. Gloria Gaither
    C. Johann Sebastian Bach
    D. Martin Luther

23. Which of these is out of chronological order?
    A. Thomas à Kempis
    B. Menno Simons
    C. Venerable Bede
    D. John Wesley

24. Which of these churches did not split into Northern and Southern branches over Civil War issues?
    A. Baptist
    B. Disciples of Christ
    C. Methodist
    D. Presbyterian

25. Which of these sports has never in the twentieth century had a committed Christian among its world champions?
    A. Figure skating
    B. The mile run
    C. Chess
    D. The decathlon

26. Of the four Presidents on Mount Rushmore, which one never joined a church?
    A. Washington
    B. Jefferson
    C. Lincoln
    D. Roosevelt

27. Which verse of "How Great Thou Art" contains a grammatical error in order to make one of the lines scan?
    A. First (O Lord my God . . .)
    B. Second (When through the woods . . .)
    C. Third (And when I think . . .)
    D. Fourth (When Christ shall come . . .)

28. Some ministers have noted that VCRs have increased their church attendance one Sunday evening each year. Which evening is usually higher now than in pre-VCR days?
    A. The fourth Sunday in January
    B. The first Sunday in July
    C. The fourth Sunday in November
    D. The fourth Sunday in December

29. In the 1660s Britain tried to control non-Anglican religions by the Conventicle Act, which forbade meetings of a certain size without official permission. What size?
    A. More than one person
    B. More than four people
    C. More than fifty people
    D. More than 144 people

30. In "Tell Me the Old, Old Story," the listener is asked to tell the story several different ways. Which of the following is not one of those ways?
    A. Sadly
    B. Simply
    C. Slowly
    D. Softly

31. An American Presbyterian minister in the 1830s advocated exercise, vegetarianism, and fresh air, saying that healthy bodies and souls went together. What food was named for him?
    A. Oysters Rockefeller
    B. Graham crackers
    C. Reuben sandwiches
    D. Sloppy Joes

32. Early Calvinists naturally wanted to know if they were part of "the elect." Calvin gave three ways to determine whether one was elect; which of the following was not a way?
    A. Being baptized
    B. Taking Communion
    C. Expressing belief in Christ
    D. Living a righteous life

33. What state is correctly matched with the nickname showing how Christians from other states felt about it in the seventeenth century?
    A. "Sin-sylvania" for Pennsylvania
    B. "Catholic Mass-achusetts" for Massachusetts
    C. "Crude York" for New York
    D. "Rogues' Island" for Rhode Island

34. William Jennings Bryan, thrice a Democratic Presidential candidate, became a Presbyterian pastor even though his parents were Baptist. Why?
    A. He had a phobia about water, so he was afraid to be immersed
    B. He thought hymns were stuffy, and the Baptists sang gospel songs instead
    C. Bryan sometimes drank wine with his meals, so his application to be a Baptist pastor was turned down
    D. He advocated "balanced Christianity," the idea that people should select a different church upon adulthood

35. The 1980 Presidential election contained much religious irony. What was unusual about the support given by most conservative Christians?
    A. They supported a candidate who, before entering politics, had been a tobacco farmer
    B. They supported a candidate who had appeared in three R-rated movies
    C. They supported a candidate who admitted in a *Playboy* interview that he had formerly been a subscriber
    D. They supported a man who rarely attended church over a man who attended regularly and taught Sunday school

36. The Council of Elvira (Middle Ages) required a
    three-year excommunication if a man broke off
    an engagement. What was unusual about that
    penalty?
    A. A woman who broke off an engage-
        ment got only six months of
        excommunication
    B. The man was not excommunicated;
        his parents were, presumably for
        bringing him up improperly
    C. The man's excommunication ended
        if he married a different woman, but
        not the same one
    D. It was the only council in church
        history, allowed to prescribe penalties,
        that was led by a woman

37. What is an "apostle spoon"?
    A. An expensive christening gift in
        fifteenth-century Italy; thus we get
        "born with a silver spoon in his
        mouth"
    B. A spoon supposedly used at the
        Last Supper; twenty-two of them
        were scattered around medieval
        Europe as relics
    C. A spoon-shaped sieve used in
        Middle Eastern archaeological digs
    D. Part of a silverware set in early
        America, called that because it was
        part of a twelve-piece set

38. "He leadeth me, O blessed thought!/O words with heavenly comfort fraught." What does "fraught" mean?
    A. Frightened (an obsolete past tense)
    B. Found
    C. Desired
    D. Filled

39. Frances Parthenope Nightingale, history's most famous Christian nurse, received her nickname from her parents' favorite city. Where is this city?
    A. Italy
    B. France
    C. England
    D. Spain

40. According to Charles Woodmason, Anglican missionary to frontier America in the 1760s, what percentage of frontier brides were pregnant on their wedding day?
    A. Thirty-four
    B. Fifty-four
    C. Seventy-four
    D. Ninety-four

41. Which president signed the bill to add the words "under God" to the Pledge of Allegiance?
    A. James Garfield
    B. Woodrow Wilson
    C. Dwight Eisenhower
    D. John Kennedy

42. "I know Jesus said man doesn't live by bread alone, but I don't remember where." How can one best locate the verse reference for this?
    A. A concordance
    B. A Bible dictionary
    C. An interlinear Greek-English text
    D. A set of Bible commentaries

43. Why was CBS news reporter Bob Keeshan honored by the Baptist media commission for "contributing to the. . .ethical growth of. . .this nation"?
    A. His special area of reporting was medical ethics, and he reported from an antiabortion point of view
    B. In addition to news reporting, he played the part of Captain Kangaroo
    C. In addition to news reporting, he played the part of Mr. Greenjeans
    D. In addition to news reporting, he played the part of Mr. Moose

44. According to the Didache (did-uh-kay, early Christian manual), how often were early Christians asked to fast?
    A. Every Saturday
    B. Every Wednesday and Friday
    C. Any time they realized they had committed a serious sin, for a period from sunup to sundown
    D. They were asked not to fast so often, for they were overdoing it

45. Who said at his martyrdom that he had served
    Christ for eighty-six years?
    A. Paul
    B. Justin Martyr
    C. Polycarp
    D. Felix Manz

46. What group did Bishop John Robinson's 1963
    book *Honest to God* encourage?
    A. The small prayer group movement
    B. Anglicans
    C. The "confessors"
    D. The death of God movement

47. What American colony was founded as a refuge
    for Quakers?
    A. Pennsylvania
    B. Rhode Island
    C. Montana
    D. Georgia

48. In A.D. 419, according to Roman law, a fugitive
    was safe if he could get within fifty feet of what?
    A. A large group of well-armed friends
    B. A priest
    C. The Eucharist (provided it had been
       consecrated)
    D. A church door

49. Theologian Lyman Beecher fathered the author of what famous book?
    A. *Hind's Feet on High Places*
    B. *The Christian's Secret of a Happy Life*
    C. *In His Steps*
    D. *Uncle Tom's Cabin*

50. What snack food was supposedly invented by a seventh-century Italian monk to reward children who memorized prayers?
    A. Popcorn
    B. Caramel corn
    C. Potato chips
    D. Pretzels

51. In England some Anglican priests took multiple churches (getting government pay for both) while serving only one. In 1750, what percent of churches had no local priest?
    A. Three
    B. Ten
    C. Thirty
    D. Fifty-five

52. What controversial 1988 movie led to a Christian boycott in many theaters?
    A. *All about Eve*
    B. *The Last Temptation of Christ*
    C. *The Satanic Verses*
    D. *Rahab*

53. What Biblical region is fittingly mentioned in the hymn "Send the Light"?
   A. Asia Minor
   B. Galatia
   C. Macedonia
   D. Crete

54. For at least a hundred years after the appearance of forks (in the eleventh century), ministers preached against using them. Why?
   A. Because the devil had a forked (cloven) hoof
   B. Since food comes from God, it should only be eaten with instruments created by God (i.e., fingers)
   C. Legend said that Eve had reached into the tree with a pitchfork to get her piece of fruit
   D. The first forks only had two tines, an unholy number; after a third tine was added, ministers approved

55. What is the religious background of contemporary Christian singer Amy Grant?
   A. Non-instrumental Churches of Christ
   B. Southern Baptist
   C. Assemblies of God
   D. Mormon

56. "How easy it would be to convert these people— and to make them work for us." What Spanish explorer made this observation about the American Indians?
   A. Christopher Columbus
   B. Hernando Cortez
   C. Cabeza de Vaca
   D. Francisco Pizarro

57. Aligheri Dante, Joan of Arc, and Queen Isabella of Spain lived in the late Middle Ages. In what order did they live?
   A. Dante, Joan, Isabella
   B. Joan, Dante, Isabella
   C. Dante, Isabella, Joan
   D. Joan, Isabella, Dante

58. About what percentage of Americans are church or synagogue members?
   A. Thirty
   B. Fifty
   C. Seventy
   D. Ninety

59. What percentage of Christians shop at Christian bookstores?
   A. Thirty
   B. Fifty
   C. Seventy
   D. Ninety

60. During what century did numerous churches for the first time begin to take a stance of total abstinence against alcohol?
   A. Fourteenth
   B. Sixteenth
   C. Eighteenth
   D. Twentieth

61. What denomination is so closely associated with cold weather that (says one writer) its strength in a state can almost be determined by the state's windchill index?
   A. Baptist
   B. Methodist
   C. Lutheran
   D. Presbyterian

62. Which of the following has not been a Communion issue over which Christians have killed one another?
   A. Should people get both bread and cup or just the cup?
   B. Should bread or a cracker be used?
   C. Does the bread contain Christ's body or merely represent Christ's body?
   D. May white grapes be used, or must they be purple grapes as in Palestine?

63. What is a "Precious Moment"?
    A. The communication time shared twice a day between spouses at a Marriage Encounter seminar
    B. The testimony time at an old-fashioned Methodist church
    C. A cute religious figurine
    D. The time of silence at the close of Quaker services when God is asked to speak to the people

64. "We have four miles of beds eighteen inches apart. We are steeped up to our necks in blood. And there are two more ships loading at the Crimea with wounded." Who is this quote from?
    A. Florence Nightingale
    B. Jenny Lind
    C. Francis of Assisi
    D. Brother Lawrence

65. Of unchurched Americans, about what percentage say they believe Jesus Christ was God?
    A. Five
    B. Twenty-five
    C. Forty-five
    D. Sixty-five

66. What percentage of all Americans say they read the Bible at least once a month?
    A. Fifteen
    B. Thirty-five
    C. Fifty-five
    D. Seventy-five

67. What percentage of Americans say they pray regularly?
    A. Twenty-five
    B. Forty-five
    C. Sixty-five
    D. Eighty-five

68. Approximately how many religious bookstores are there in the U.S.?
    A. 800
    B. 3,000
    C. 8,000
    D. 30,000

69. Of unchurched Americans, what percentage say they have made a "commitment to Christ"?
    A. Eighteen
    B. Thirty-eight
    C. Fifty-eight
    D. Seventy-eight

70. When Jonathan Edwards took on his first ministry, he had big shoes to fill. The previous minister, Solomon Stoddard, had what claim to fame?
    A. He had preached 3,000 Sundays in a row without missing a single scheduled sermon
    B. He had received more than twenty-five marriage proposals, but turned them all down to focus on God
    C. He had memorized all of Paul's epistles plus the book of Luke
    D. Being a wealthy farmer, every Sunday he conspicuously returned all his salary to the offering plate

71. Roger Williams was expelled from Massachusetts for several reasons, one of which was he felt it was a sin to take the Indians' land. What was Governor Winthrop's response to this?
    A. If God didn't want us to take over, why did He make room for us by sending smallpox to kill the Indians?
    B. God created animals and white people but not Indians. It's our job to get the animals' land back for them
    C. In two thousand years the Indians haven't built a single church here; they don't deserve this land
    D. This is good land; it would be poor stewardship not to take it

72. When the American Constitutional Convention was deadlocked, which delegate suggested praying to God for wisdom?
    A. Benjamin Franklin
    B. John Hancock
    C. George Washington
    D. Thomas Jefferson

73. Which of these hymns is based upon the episode of the woman at the well?
    A. "More about Jesus"
    B. "Fill My Cup, Lord"
    C. "Reach out to Jesus"
    D. "Lord, I Want to Be a Christian"

74. Churches were at the forefront of prison reform in mid-nineteenth-century England. Which of the following was a much-needed reform, becoming law in 1856?
    A. Prisoners no longer had an ear notched for each jail term
    B. The straw in the mattresses was changed every ten days (to cut down on the number of bedbugs)
    C. Jailers were given salaries
    D. Prisoners could receive visits from family members

75. What group produced during World War I the booklet "Hand-to-Hand Fighting" ("I could see Jesus himself. . .running a bayonet through an enemy's body")?
    A. Southern Baptist Convention
    B. The Mennonite Armed Forces Committee
    C. United Methodist Church Sunday School Board
    D. Young Men's Christian Association (YMCA)

76. What best-selling novel was written in the early twentieth century by Disciples of Christ minister Harold Bell Wright?
    A. *In His Steps*
    B. *Christy*
    C. *The Shepherd of the Hills*
    D. *The Curate's Daughter*

77. Some ministers in colonial New England refused infant baptism to infants born on a Sunday. Why?
    A. These infants were considered holier, so they didn't need baptism
    B. It was considered that they had broken the Sabbath by being born on Sunday
    C. Their mothers were ostracized for laboring on a Sunday
    D. People felt birth and conception occurred on the same weekday; parents were punished for having sex on Sunday

78. In the early 1980s psychologists John Vokey and Don Read studied "backmasking" (alleged practice of putting Satanic messages backwards on albums). What did they find?
    A. That people can understand Satanic messages backwards, but not Christian ones
    B. That people cannot understand backward messages at all
    C. That people can understand Christian messages backwards, but not Satanic ones
    D. That people can understand all backward messages

79. In A.D. 70 an event occurred that tended to loosen the church from its Jewish roots. What event?
    A. A law was passed in Rome forbidding Saturday worship
    B. The first widespread persecution of Christians by Jews began
    C. The Temple was destroyed
    D. The New Testament was completed in this year, so the Old Testament was relegated to a lower place

80. Complete this quote by Marshall Lucas: God doesn't always smooth the path—
    A. But tears of sorrow soothe His wrath
    B. Especially when His will is for us to be traveling a nearby blacktop
    C. But sometimes He puts springs in the wagon
    D. For often a rough path is what we need to smooth us

81. What is often considered to be the oldest known Christian writing outside the New Testament, dating to perhaps A.D. 90?
    A. I Clement
    B. The Epistle of Ignatius to Smyrna
    C. The Epistle of Thomas
    D. The Testimony of Justin Martyr

82. This writing (from the previous question) contains several interesting features, including all of the following except which?
    A. An observation that the local church had more than one bishop
    B. The earliest reference to the martyrdoms of Peter and Paul
    C. The statement that the Lord's Supper should be served only by elders
    D. A reprimand to a church that had allowed two women to serve as elders

83. Several books have been written on the problems of a Christian wife living with an unbelieving husband. When did the first booklet on this subject appear?
    A. Around 200
    B. Around 1400
    C. Around 1800
    D. Surprisingly, not until 1954

84. According to the hymn, which of the following will occur if you "count your many blessings"?
    A. You'll begin to smile
    B. Angels will come to comfort you
    C. You'll cheer up others who are burdened
    D. You'll need to borrow a calculator

85. Which of the following is the correct title of an influential book by Fritz Ridenour?
    A. *How to Be a Christian without Really Trying*
    B. *How to Be a Christian without Being Religious*
    C. *How to Be a Christian without Being Obnoxious*
    D. *How to Be a Christian without Theology*

86. Medieval Bible study was not very scholarly. As an example, who did the well-educated theologian Bonaventura say wrote the Book of Psalms?
    A. Adam
    B. Noah
    C. Jesus
    D. Mary

87. In 1650 Quaker founder George Fox was sentenced to six months in an English jail for blasphemy. What had he said to bring about this sentence?
    A. If God hath actually predestined certain human beings to hell, then He is more evil than Satan
    B. The age of miracles hath not passed; the Holy Ghost worketh miracles this very day and hour
    C. Christ has taken away my sin
    D. Jesus loves me

88. How many churches are we aware of that were recorded in the New Testament or in other contemporary sources by A.D. 100?
    A. 12
    B. 42
    C. 112
    D. 242

89. Roger Bacon, a thirteenth-century friar, was probably the greatest scientist of his century. What was his scientific goal?
    A. To find evidence for the Genesis account of creation that would prove evolution false
    B. To determine exactly where heaven was located
    C. To help the pope develop a weapon that would kill all Moslems and thus bring peace to the world
    D. To determine if the relic at Canterbury was indeed the clay left over after God made Adam

90. Why were love feasts forbidden by the church in the fourth century?
    A. The "love" involved had come to be directed toward the opposite sex more often than toward God
    B. People were overeating and feeling stuffed all afternoon
    C. Often they led to episodes of drunkenness
    D. Now that Christianity was accepted by the Roman Empire, all secret rituals were abandoned

91. "Don't praise yourself; let others do it!" What version of Proverbs 27:2 is this?
    A. Living
    B. New International
    C. New King James
    D. Phillips

92. George Herbert's poem "Mary/Army: An Anagram" is only two lines long. What follows this opening line: "How well her name an army doth present"?
    A. She hath about her life a heavenly scent!
    B. For in her the Messiah makes descent!
    C. The heavenly Sword to her hath now been lent!
    D. In whom the Lord of Hosts did pitch his tent!

93. What is the "Johannine comma"?
    A. There was no comma in Koine Greek until John invented it for use in his Gospel
    B. John had commas in his original manuscript to mark off verse divisions
    C. In I John 5:7 words were added to manuscripts, and are still found in the King James Version, to "prove" the Trinity
    D. John Calvin had Bible translators in Geneva whipped for every omitted comma to increase accuracy

94. Which of these last names indicates that the person had an ancestor who was ordained?
    A. Clark
    B. Wilburn
    C. Swaim
    D. Donahue

95. What was the date of the first complete New Testament canon (list of books) as we have it today?
    A. 167
    B. 267
    C. 367
    D. 467

96. The Nicene Creed, composed about A.D. 325, said Christ was "Very God of Very God, of one substance with the Father." What was unusual about this creed?
    A. It was the first creed ever
    B. It was the first creed ever to contain nonbiblical language in any significant way
    C. It was the first creed to carry an automatic death penalty for people refusing to say it
    D. It was the first creed to split the church

97. In the Renaissance many people believed it to be
   for the best that Adam and Eve sinned, because
   otherwise we'd never have known the extent of
   God's mercy. What is this called?
   A. The excellent expulsion
   B. The fortunate fall
   C. The purifying punishment
   D. The gateway of grace

98. In the Apocryphal book Bel and the Dragon,
   Daniel proves the priests of Bel are eating the
   food offerings, not the false god. How does
   Daniel prove it?
   A. He scatters ashes on the floor to
       reveal their footprints
   B. He has threads around the food
       triggered to an alarm system
   C. He has the priests locked into Bel's
       temple for thirty days and shows that
       they don't starve
   D. He sets out blueberries, and the next
       day the priests all have blue tongues

99. The religious poem (and song) "The Touch of the
   Master's Hand" compares our lives before Christ
   to what?
   A. An old musical instrument
   B. A worn-out pair of gloves
   C. Broken pieces of chalk
   D. The back of a slave who's been
       whipped

100. Julian of Norwich, in her most famous vision, held a small nutlike object; asking God what it was, she heard Him say, "Everything that has been made." What happened next?

    A. Julian said, "It looks so fragile. What keeps it from breaking"? God replied, "I love it"

    B. The nut crumbled to powder, and God said, "This is what will happen unless you convince people to repent"

    C. Julian asked, "How large are you compared to this"? God said, "Once I shed a single tear, and it flooded"

    D. Julian discovered a worm inside and understood what Satan had done to the universe

101. One of Hudson Taylor's most significant contributions to missions work was his hairstyle. What did he wear?

    A. An Afro

    B. A pigtail

    C. A ponytail

    D. A crew cut

102. What two books of the Bible were joined until 1448?

    A. Judges and Ruth

    B. Ezra and Nehemiah

    C. Proverbs and Ecclesiastes

    D. Jeremiah and Lamentations

103. What Christian songwriter is famous for lines like: "I woke up Monday mornin'/ My head all full of nothin'/ I walked down to McDonald's/To get me a Egg McMuffin"?
    A. Carman
    B. Stormie Omartian
    C. Bill Gaither
    D. Anne Herring

104. Many of our months come from the names of Roman gods at the time of Christ. Which of the following months is not named after a Roman god?
    A. January
    B. March
    C. June
    D. July

105. Baptist church origins are usually traced back to the baptism of John Smith in 1608. Since there were no other Baptists around, who baptized him?
    A. He baptized himself
    B. He prayed, and God showed him a nearby waterfall, which he took as God's method of baptizing him
    C. He was converted during a shipwreck and went under three times without drowning; he called that a baptism
    D. His wife baptized him, and then he baptized her

106. Tertullian wrote a tract discussing the problems of a Christian wife married to a pagan husband. To whom did he dedicate the tract?
    A.   His daughter
    B.   His mother
    C.   His wife
    D.   Paula, the wife of a pagan Roman senator

107. In 1961 a stone was found at Caesarea with the name of a Bible character on it. Scholars had argued about the existence of this character for years. What character?
    A.   Job
    B.   Jonah
    C.   Salome
    D.   Portius Pilate

108. When Origen, the first great Biblical scholar, was asked in the third century who wrote the book of Hebrews, what was his answer?
    A.   Apollos
    B.   Aquila and Priscilla
    C.   Paul
    D.   Only God knows

109. What are Inklings?
    A. Prophecies not understood until after
       they occur
    B. Children in the Assemblies of God
       who've memorized at least a thou-
       sand Bible verses
    C. C. S. Lewis's fellowship group
    D. Manuscripts that have been erased
       and written over; with ultraviolet
       light we can now see the original

110. In the fifth century Augustine made a list of con-
     temporary heresies. How many did he come up
     with?
    A. Eight
    B. Eighty-eight
    C. 888
    D. None. All the heretics had now
       been killed

SECTION 3

1. Three of the following are punch lines from well-known "sermon jokes." Which one is not?
   A. Is there anyone else up there who can help me?
   B. I sent you two boats and a helicopter; what more do you want?
   C. The man was so relieved he said, "Praise the Lord!"
   D. That was no lady; that was the preacher's wife!

2. One of the great religious works of all time is Blaise Pascal's *Pensées*. What is its title in English?
   A. Writings
   B. Gatherings
   C. Elements
   D. Thoughts

3. When Gregory the Great became pope around 600, what did he take as his customary title?
   A. Most Potent of Potentates
   B. The Voice of God
   C. Key-Keeper
   D. Servant to the Servants of God

4. What did medieval theology students use for textbooks?
   A. They bought books just like today, except the books were hand-copied
   B. They memorized textbooks by setting the words to music
   C. They copied down the textbook words as professors read them aloud
   D. They didn't use textbooks at all; only after graduating did a theology student begin his reading

5. What was standard church practice in 400 regarding ordination of slaves?
   A. It was forbidden
   B. Theoretically, it was permissible; practically, no slave had the education to be ordained, anyway
   C. If an owner didn't want his slave ordained, the church ordained him anyway and provided compensation
   D. An owner could prevent his slave's ordination, but it was a venial sin and added 2,400 years in purgatory

6. What close friend did C. S. Lewis describe as "the ugliest man I ever met"?
   A. Warren Lewis, his brother
   B. T. S. Eliot
   C. J. R. R. Tolkien
   D. Charles Williams

7. When a playing-card maker in Geneva criticized John Calvin, what did Calvin make him do?
   A. Walk around the town without any pants on
   B. Become a Catholic
   C. Eat an entire suit from one of his decks of cards
   D. Apologize and ask Calvin to pray to God to forgive him

8. What did Henry IV say when he switched from Protestant to Catholic to become king of France?
   A. "Easy come, easy go"
   B. "Paris is well worth a mass"
   C. "I shall do so much for God that He will not care a franc"
   D. "Luther is dead; the pope is alive. Which do you think will come to my aid when necessary"?

9. Approximately when did Koine Greek, the language of the New Testament, die out?
   A. Within a decade after the completion of Revelation, due to Catullus's proclamation that everyone speak Latin
   B. The third century A.D.
   C. Shortly after Rome fell, around A.D. 500.
   D. It hasn't died out; it's still the common language of Greece and a few Mediterranean islands

10. Who conducted a scientific experiment to deter-
    mine that over 30,000 people at a time could hear
    evangelist George Whitefield's voice?
    A. Benjamin Franklin
    B. John Wesley
    C. Edward Jenner
    D. Sir Isaac Newton

11. Of what tribe of North American Indians did a
    single Franciscan friar baptize 200,000 in ten
    years, including 14,000 in one day?
    A. Aztecs
    B. Navajo
    C. Apaches
    D. Nez Perce

12. Ulfilas (early 300s) was probably the first mis-
    sionary to create an alphabet for an oral language
    to translate the Bible. For what barbarians did he
    do this?
    A. Goths
    B. Huns
    C. Vikings
    D. Cowboys

13. Speaking of Ulfilas, he deliberately left six books out of the Bible—the Samuels, Kings, and Chronicles. Why?
    A. He thought they were just plain too boring to include
    B. In the early fourth century, controversy was raging over whether these books were divinely inspired
    C. He wanted the barbarians to be more peaceful, and he thought these books encouraged war
    D. They were too difficult to translate at the current level of scholarship

14. On what American monument can one find the Old Testament quote, "Proclaim liberty throughout all the land unto all the inhabitants thereof"?
    A. The St. Louis Gateway Arch
    B. The Lincoln Memorial
    C. The Statue of Liberty
    D. The Liberty Bell

15. For what offense was John Bunyan (author of *The Pilgrim's Progress*) given a twelve-year jail term?
    A. Preaching without a license
    B. Baptizing without a license
    C. Refusing to pay taxes to support the Anglican Church
    D. Writing a boring book

16. What is the Christian significance of Kenny Price, Roy Clark, Buck Owens, and "Grandpa" Jones?
    A. They were all professors of New Testament at Fuller Seminary in the 1970s
    B. They formed a group called The Hee-Haw Gospel Quartet
    C. They led a Christian movement against Idi Amin in Uganda and were expelled from that country
    D. They have no Christian significance. They're just celebrities

17. Why does Brazil speak Portuguese while most of South America speaks Spanish?
    A. In 1493, the pope gave Brazil to Portugal and the rest of South America to Spain
    B. Originally Brazil spoke Spanish, but Portuguese priests converted the natives and won their allegiance
    C. Originally the continent spoke Portuguese, but Spanish priests won most countries' allegiance
    D. The War of the Virgin Mary (1498–1501) enabled the Portuguese to rebel on both continents

18. To teach Indians about hell, what did one Spanish friar regularly roast in a portable oven?
    A. Roast beef for an "agape" meal
    B. Live cats and dogs
    C. Clay, to show how it hardened
    D. Cheese, to show how it melted

19. What people in the early church had their deaths celebrated as "birthdays in eternity"?
    A. Martyrs
    B. Saints
    C. All Christians
    D. Those who had been born outside the church

20. What American President died the same day as C. S. Lewis?
    A. Benjamin Harrison
    B. Warren Harding
    C. John Kennedy
    D. Richard Nixon

21. Pride, greed, gluttony, lust, anger, despair. Which of the original Seven Deadly Sins is missing?
    A. Murder
    B. Foolishness
    C. Disbelief
    D. Sloth

22. When introduced to the pope, what did St. Louis baseball catcher Joe Garagiola allegedly say?
    A. "I helped win the World Series this year. Did you get anything accomplished"?
    B. "Your Holiness, I'm a Cardinal"
    C. "Your Holiness, can I have your autograph"?
    D. "Would you like my autograph"?

23. In the early 1500s, Anabaptist leader Felix Manz practiced adult baptism. How did Reformation leader Ulrich Zwingli have him punished?
    A. A fine
    B. Exile
    C. Hanging
    D. Drowning

24. Why was Corrie ten Boom released from her concentration camp just before everyone was executed?
    A. A German guard she had converted let her escape
    B. She prayed that God would "blind their eyes" and she was able to walk out unhindered
    C. There was a clerical error
    D. She wasn't released; she hid in the back of a van (in an empty ammo box) to escape

25. What is the unusual feature about the hymn "Faith of Our Fathers"?
    A. It was originally written as "Faith of Our Mothers," but was changed to make it alliterate
    B. It was written as an anti-Protestant hymn, but is now sung more often by Protestants than Catholics
    C. The fifth verse is omitted from our hymnals because it says children must be beaten "till they have faith"
    D. The author, Frederick Faber, wrote no other hymns; he was a pencil manufacturer

26. With what teaching is Robert Schuller most closely identified?
    A. Signs and wonders
    B. Ecumenism
    C. Form criticism
    D. Self-esteem

27. What important Christian work contains the characters Slubgob, Wormwood, and Glubose?
    A. *The Pilgrim's Progress*
    B. The Last Will and Testament of the Springfield Presbytery
    C. *The Screwtape Letters*
    D. The Bible

28. For what alleged miracle was Bernard canonized as a saint?
    A. While he was adoring a statue of Mary, its breasts dripped milk onto his lips
    B. While he was adoring a statue of John the Baptist, it poured water on his head
    C. While he was adoring a statue of Jesus, it bled onto his hands
    D. While he was adoring a statue of Samson, it hit him on the side of the head with a donkey jawbone

29. Speaking of Bernard, what was unusual about his decision to become a monk?
    A. There were no monks; he was the first
    B. Thirty male relatives tried to talk him out of it; instead, he convinced all of them to become monks, too
    C. Because of his alleged miracle, he was actually canonized before becoming a monk
    D. He was married

30. What recurrent physical problem did Martin Luther claim was caused by his days as a monk?
    A. Frequent migraine headaches
    B. Infertility
    C. Backache
    D. Constipation

31. What is the tonsure (monk's haircut) intended to represent?
    A. Christ's crown of thorns
    B. The halo the monk will have if canonized
    C. The halo the monk will have in heaven
    D. The bald spot stands for a pure heart; the surrounding hair stands for a sinful body

32. What did Francis of Assisi allegedly yell when his clothes caught fire and someone tried to put it out?
    A. "Don't hurt the fire!"
    B. "Hurry! Help Brother Shirt!"
    C. "Brother Fire, shame on you!"
    D. "Stay away! I'm a sinner! I deserve to burn!"

33. Which of the following is not one of John Wesley's "Rules for Singing"?
    A. Do not raise your hands while singing; only your voice
    B. Do not sing as if you were half dead
    C. Sing modestly; do not bawl
    D. Take care not to sing too slowly

34. What was the first children's religious album to "go gold" (500,000 sales)?
    A. *The Music Machine*
    B. *Bullfrogs and Butterflies*
    C. *Bullfrogs and Butterflies, Part II*
    D. *Jesus Loves Me Today!*

35. In the early 1500s, the Bishop of Constance absolved Swiss priests of fornication if they did what?
    A. Left the priesthood and married
    B. Said ten "Hail Mary's" for each offense
    C. Paid a fine of four guilders for each child they sired
    D. Promised not to become involved with nuns or wives

36. Identify this book—114 chapters, published in 1486, over 400 different editions, generally considered the second most important book in Christian history (next to the Bible):
    A. *The City of God*
    B. *The Imitation of Christ*
    C. *A Serious Call to a Devout and Holy Life*
    D. *Joni*

37. How was dancing frequently described in the mid-twentieth century by conservative church members?
    A. "The devil's playground"
    B. "Animal behavior best left in the jungle"
    C. "Lascivious, licentious, lewd, and lustful"
    D. "A vertical expression of a horizontal idea"

38. What document says people are "endowed by their Creator with certain unalienable Rights"?
    A. The Declaration of Independence
    B. The Declaration of the Rights of Man
    C. The Preamble to the Constitution
    D. The Bill of Rights

39. In the late 1700s, while preparing for his later mission work in India, William Carey studied Latin, Hebrew, Dutch, and Italian. What did his wife Dorothy study, and why?
    A. Hindi—she wanted to know something useful
    B. Greek—she wanted to translate the New Testament
    C. The same languages as William—she wanted the two of them to share as many experiences as possible
    D. English—she was illiterate

40. What daughter of a famous pastor was described by Lincoln as "the little lady who made this big war"?
    A. Queen Victoria
    B. Anne Boleyn
    C. Harriet Beecher Stowe
    D. Susan B. Anthony

41. To what prayer of Ruth Graham's (as a teenager) did her sister respond by praying, "Lord, don't listen to her"?
    A. "Lord, please let Billy like me"
    B. "Lord, please let me be beheaded"
    C. "Lord, please cause all of us girls to marry preachers"
    D. "Lord, please make my sister perfect"

42. The refrain of a Fanny Crosby hymn ends with "Let us hope and trust, Let us watch and pray, And labor till the Master comes." What is the first part of that refrain?
    A. "We will work with each other, We will work side by side"
    B. "Toiling on, toiling on, toiling on, toiling on, Toiling on, toiling on, toiling on, toiling on"
    C. "So do what we must, We'll work night and day, Until cold Death our heart benumbs"
    D. "Praise the Lord, Praise the Lord"

43. Why was Augustine so flabbergasted the first time he ever saw Ambrose (the man who converted him) reading?
    A. Ambrose read without moving his lips
    B. Augustine had never seen anyone read the Bible before
    C. Augustine had never seen a Christian read anything else besides the Bible
    D. Even though alone, Ambrose was reading out loud

44. When Philip of Hesse wanted to end his marriage and marry another woman, what was Martin Luther's controversial advice?
    A. As head of his wife, Philip had the right to kill her and marry another
    B. Philip could get a divorce without the consent of the Catholic Church
    C. Philip should send his wife into exile and marry the other woman
    D. Divorce was wrong, so Philip should commit bigamy

45. Approximately how many sermons did John Wesley preach?
    A. 5,000
    B. 10,000
    C. 20,000
    D. 40,000

46. What was probably the most significant event, spiritually speaking, on the continent of Europe in the eighteenth century?
    A. The Baptist denomination was founded
    B. The modern Pentecostal movement began to take shape in Bohemia
    C. Lisbon, Portugal, had an earthquake
    D. Rome, Italy, had a flood

47. Why did Robert Goulet and Tony Bennett have their concerts canceled at Robert Schuller's Crystal Cathedral?
    A. Schuller had discovered that some of the songs they sing are negative
    B. Schuller did not want secular music sung in the church
    C. It was discovered that Goulet was a Mormon and Bennett a Moslem
    D. The Crystal Cathedral had had so many secular concerts that it lost tax-exempt status

48. What Puritan brothers had names meaning "to grow greater" and "cloth-producing plant"?
    A. The Williamses
    B. The Mathers
    C. The Fletchers
    D. The Billingsleys

49. Which early church father thought the church should kill heretics?
    A. Justin Martyr
    B. Tertullian
    C. Athanasius
    D. Augustine

50. When the famous fourth-century preacher John Chrysostom said, "Her mouth is like a bear's mouth dyed with blood," what evil woman was he describing?
    A. Any woman wearing lipstick
    B. A prostitute
    C. Jezebel
    D. Aphrodite

51. How did the "black-bumper Mennonites" of early twentieth-century America get their name?
    A. They closed their eyes when they saw sin, bumped into things, and got their eyes blackened
    B. They would own cars only if all the chrome was painted black
    C. When they met a black man, they would bump him for having the "curse of Cain"
    D. They would not flavor their coffee with cream or sugar ("bumper" being a mug of coffee)

52. The name of what religious season comes from the Latin for "to come"?
    A. Easter
    B. Advent
    C. Christmas
    D. The Fourth of July

53. What did Donald Thomas, a Brooklyn minister, do from September 18–22, 1978?
    A. Preached history's longest sermon
    B. Picketed a nuclear weapons site
    C. Singlehandedly sang all the parts in twelve Christmas cantatas
    D. Prayed nonstop

54. What famous European church building was begun the year Columbus sailed, took 120 years to complete, and covers 18,110 square yards?
    A. Notre Dame
    B. Westminster Cathedral
    C. St. Peter's in Rome
    D. St. Sofia's

55. What obscure apostle did Danny Thomas admire enough to name a children's hospital after him?
    A. Thaddeus
    B. Simon the Zealot
    C. Barabbas
    D. Jude

56. When Quaker founder George Fox refused to take off his hat in King Charles II's presence, what did Charles do?
    A. Took off his own headgear
    B. Beheaded Fox, calling it poetic justice
    C. Prayed to God to strike Fox dead for insolence
    D. Said he wished his soldiers had half the gumption Fox did

57. When medieval scholar Thomas Aquinas was asked what he most thanked God for, what did he reply?
    A. "Jesus loves me"
    B. "I know everything worth knowing"
    C. "I have understood every page I have ever read"
    D. "I have never had to work for a living like a common peasant"

58. What activity was the monk engaged in who complained, "Thin ink, bad vellum, difficult text"?
    A. Scripture memorization
    B. Preparing a sermon
    C. Writing a master's thesis
    D. Copying manuscripts

59. When a New England church choir went on strike, what verse of "Marching to Zion" did the minister ask them to lead the congregation in?
    A. Come, we that love the Lord and let our joys be known
    B. Let those refuse to sing who never knew our God
    C. The hill of Zion yields a thousand sacred sweets
    D. Then let our songs abound and every tear be dry

60. Which of the following is not true of John and Elizabeth Bunyan's marriage (John being the author of *The Pilgrim's Progress*)?
    A. He spent eleven of the first thirteen years of their marriage in jail
    B. He was thirty-one and she was sixteen or seventeen when they married
    C. He had four children by a previous marriage, and she had been their baby-sitter
    D. They were so poor they did not have "a dish or spoon betwixt us both"

61. From about 1965–1995, which of these groups grew by over 1,000 percent?
    A. The Nazarenes
    B. The Assemblies of God
    C. The Church of God in Christ
    D. The Church of God (Cleveland, Tennessee)

62. What was John Scopes accused of in the Dayton, Tennessee, "Monkey Trial"?
    A. Cruelty to monkeys
    B. Trying to make a monkey out of local pastor Smith Wigglesworth
    C. Teaching evolution
    D. Teaching evolution without giving equal time to creation

63. When Charles Spurgeon assumed his first pastorate, what gift did he receive from the deacons, and why?
    A. A wife, because being married was one of the conditions for being a minister there
    B. A new horse, for his old nag had caused him to be late to both trial sermons
    C. White handkerchiefs, because the one he used during services was blue with polka dots
    D. An entire Bible, because he had been too poor to afford more than a New Testament

64. Why were early Christian martyrs sometimes wrapped in animal skins?
    A. So dogs would attack them
    B. Because in Communion they "ate flesh and drank blood"
    C. To show they were "children of the Lamb"
    D. To show they were no better than beasts

65. What missionary wrote, "No one knows the value of water till he is deprived of it . . . I have drunk water with rhinoceros urine and buffaloes' dung"?
    A. David Livingstone
    B. Hudson Taylor
    C. Henry David Thoreau
    D. Jim Elliott

66. What is the subtitle of The Florida Boys' southern gospel hit "When He Was on the Cross"?
    A. "Then He Removed My Dross"
    B. "He Cancelled Out My Loss"
    C. "I Was on His Mind"
    D. "Love Was on Its Way"

67. Early Christians preferred to baptize in "living water." What did they mean by that?
    A. Running water (such as a stream)
    B. Water blessed by a bishop
    C. Liquid water (as opposed to steam or ice)
    D. Hot (or at least warm) water

68. What king's death led to the birth of John Wesley?
    A. Charlemagne
    B. William of Orange
    C. George III
    D. Saul

69. Who said, in reference to his wife's homemaking
    abilities, "In domestic affairs I defer to Katie.
    Otherwise, I am led by the Holy Ghost"?
    A. Martin Luther
    B. John Calvin
    C. Pope Paul VI
    D. Thomas Campbell

70. What was Polycarp's response when asked to
    blaspheme and escape being a martyr?
    A. "No way"
    B. "If thou bringest the beasts, the fire,
       the scourge, and the sword, I shalt
       honor Him through them all"
    C. "Jesus Christ did never speak
       against me"
    D. "How can I speak evil of my King
       who saved me"?

71. What, originally, was a "devil's advocate"?
    A. Originally, Judas; it came to mean
       any supposed friend who betrays us
    B. A heretic; a person who twisted
       Scripture to get a different meaning
    C. A person assigned to prove that
       someone should not become a saint
       in the Catholic Church
    D. Originally, it was rum; it came to be
       applied to any alcoholic beverage

72. Whose collected prayers include a request for blessing on his (successful) attempt to compose the first major dictionary of the English language?
    A. John Samuelson
    B. Samuel Johnson
    C. Noah Webster
    D. Daniel Webster

73. In 1790 Philadelphia Quakers provided a building where people who needed to repent were made to meditate alone on Scripture. What was this experiment called?
    A. A confessional
    B. A judiciary
    C. A medical center
    D. A penitentiary

74. What Watergate participant has become a leader in prison ministry?
    A. Richard Nixon
    B. Chuck Colson
    C. H. R. Haldeman
    D. G. Gordon Liddy

75. What famous evangelist often ended his preaching by quoting the poem "Slide, Kelly, Slide," in allusion to his major-league record of ninety-five stolen bases in one season?
    A. Billy Graham
    B. Billy Sunday
    C. "Wahoo" Sam Crawford
    D. Ty Cobb

76. What early religion competed with Christianity for supremacy and, remarkably, centered around an incarnation, resurrection, baptism, communion, and final judgment?
    A. Mithraism
    B. Zoroastrianism
    C. Platonism
    D. Schismism

77. What was Friar Luca Pacioli's contribution to the world of business?
    A. He invented the tax deduction
    B. He put together the theology that allowed Christians to loan money to fellow Christians at interest
    C. He set forth the first theology of capitalism
    D. He invented double-entry bookkeeping

78. What do Noah's beard, Mary's milk, and Joseph's breath have in common?
    A. They were all white
    B. They were all warm
    C. They were all alleged relics contained in medieval churches
    D. They were found last year in a cave in Israel, neatly labeled and in a remarkable state of preservation

79. After Constantine became a Christian, whose faces did he have put on Roman coins?
    A. Apostles such as Paul and Peter
    B. Roman gods such as Mars and Jupiter
    C. Family members such as himself and his wife
    D. Contemporary bishops such as Athanasius and Malodorous

80. What was the most significant Christian event of A.D. 1000?
    A. Jesus did not return
    B. Charlemagne was crowned the first Holy Roman emperor
    C. The Moslems were defeated at the Battle of Tours, thus keeping Europe Christian
    D. The term "pope" was used for the first time

81. What group, founded by Ignatius Loyola, were taught to view their bodies as "ulcerous sores"?
    A. Jesuits
    B. Benedictines
    C. Franciscans
    D. Brothers of Leprosy

82. What New England state was called, for its religious freedom, "the sink into which all the rest of the colonies empty their heretics"?
    A. Massachusetts
    B. Connecticut
    C. New Hampshire
    D. Rhode Island

83. Who was the first famous American novelist of Christian romances?
    A. Janette Oke
    B. Eugenia Price
    C. Grace Livingston Hill
    D. Marian Wells

84. Who was the plaintiff in the 1963 Supreme Court decision banning prayer in public schools?
    A. Madelyn Murray O'Hair
    B. Clarence Darrow
    C. The state of Texas
    D. William J. Murray III

85. What missionary hymn describing places to carry the gospel was written in fifteen minutes?
    A. "In Christ There Is No East or West"
    B. "From Greenland's Icy Mountains"
    C. "Fling Out the Banner"
    D. "Send the Light"

86. Because thirteenth-century saint Clare could allegedly see things happen across town, what modern invention is she the patron saint of?
    A. Television
    B. VCRs
    C. Binoculars
    D. Telescopes

87. When the British Association met to discuss evolution in 1860, what insulting question did Bishop Wilberforce ask T. H. Huxley?
    A. "If apes turned into human beings, why do we still have apes"?
    B. "Did you descend from an ape on your grandfather's side or your grandmother's"?
    C. "The rest of us are having roast beef for luncheon today. Would you prefer bananas"?
    D. "Do you wish the lamps turned down? I suppose cave-dwellers such as yourself have weak eyes"

88. Who first called religion the opium of the people?
    A. Thomas de Quincey
    B. Abou ben Adam
    C. Karl Marx
    D. Adolph Hitler

89. The Revised Standard Version of the Bible has just under 1,000,000 words. Approximately how many words are in the *Reader's Digest* condensed version?
    A. 800,000
    B. 600,000
    C. 400,000
    D. 200,000

90. What occurs during an auto-da-fe ceremony?
    A. "Holy water" is placed on automobiles
    B. Feet are washed and anointed with oil
    C. After the death of an unbelieving spouse, the surviving husband or wife prays for them
    D. Heretics are burned

91. What were the Salvation Army's female preachers in the nineteenth century known as?
    A. The Hallelujah Lasses
    B. The Praise the Lord Preachers
    C. The Holy Hannahs
    D. The Righteous Rahabs

92. How many pieces of glass are in a square yard of medieval religious mosaics?
    A. 2,000
    B. 12,000
    C. 32,000
    D. 52,000

93. Why did fourth-century bishop John Chrysostom go two years without lying down?
    A. Because he wasn't tired
    B. Because he took literally Peter's words about standing firm in God's grace
    C. Because Jesus had said "Watch and pray," and he wanted to do a good job of it
    D. When he was deposed by a rival bishop, he said, "I'm not going to take this lying down," and he didn't

94. In the hymn "All Hail the Power of Jesus' Name," which of these is not a rhyming line with "And crown Him Lord of all"?
    A. "Hear heav'nly music call"
    B. "On this terrestrial ball"
    C. "Ye ransomed from the fall"
    D. "We at His feet may fall!"

95. What is the English name for the Crusader whose French title was "Coeur-de-Lion"?
    A. Henry
    B. Richard
    C. Edward
    D. James

96. To what TV preacher did the following 1980s joke allude? "Did you hear that _____ died yesterday"? "No, what happened"? "One of the checks made out to him bounced!"
    A. Jim Bakker
    B. Oral Roberts
    C. Rex Humbard
    D. Jerry Falwell

97. What book in the Bible did Martin Luther condemn by saying, "It reveals nothing"?
    A. Numbers
    B. Song of Solomon
    C. Jude
    D. Revelation

98. Which of the following is not one of the Chronicles of Narnia, the enormously popular Christian fantasy series for children?
    A. *The Silver Chair*
    B. *The Queen's Secret*
    C. *The Last Battle*
    D. *The Horse and His Boy*

99. Frances Havergal, writer of "I Gave My Life for Thee," disliked the poem and threw it into the fireplace (where a fire was blazing) to burn it. How do we still have it today?
    A. Allegedly, the fire would not burn it; she took its preservation as a sign that God wanted it saved
    B. She immediately changed her mind and suffered second-degree burns on her right hand and arm retrieving it
    C. That night she had a dream that she should rewrite the poem
    D. She missed the fire; her father was cleaning up the fireplace, found the poem, and saved it

100. What religious term has been playfully defined as "getting to know the opposite sects"?
    A. Evangelicalism
    B. Fundamentalism
    C. Ecumenism
    D. Interderogatoryianism

101. In the 1970s, what percentage of the world's Protestant missionaries came from North America?
    A. Ten percent
    B. Thirty percent
    C. Fifty percent
    D. Seventy percent

102. Pope Gregory declared of certain slave boys in Italy that they appeared to be "not Angles, but Angels," so he encouraged missionaries to visit their country. What country?
    A. Sweden
    B. Germany
    C. England
    D. Norway

103. In what century was the word "catholic" first used to describe the general (as opposed to local) church?
    A. Second
    B. Fourth
    C. Sixth
    D. Eighth

104. There were three prerequisites for receiving Communion around A.D. 150, according to Justin Martyr. Which of the following was not a listed prerequisite?
    A. Belief
    B. Baptism
    C. Moral purity
    D. Correct theology

105. Which of the following is "Silent Night" in Spanish?
    A. "Alla en el Pesebre"
    B. "Oid un Son en Alta Esfera"
    C. "Noche de Paz"
    D. "Pastores cerca de Belen"

106. Twelfth-century Cistercian monasteries celebrated Christmas by doing something they weren't allowed to do any other day of the year. What was that?
    A. Eat meat
    B. Heat their buildings
    C. Take a bath
    D. Visit their families

107. "Only the Chancellor steadfast in fight/ Watches o'er Germany by day and night/ Always caring for us." This is the Nazi version for which Christmas carol?
    A. "Joy to the World"
    B. "O Little Town of Bethlehem"
    C. "Carol of the Bells"
    D. "Silent Night"

108. What is the title of the all-time best-selling a cappella Christmas album?
    A. "An Evening in December"
    B. "Vocal Joy"
    C. "Yuletide Harmonies"
    D. "An Acappella Christmas"

109. In *The Best Christmas Pageant Ever,* what unusual gift do the Wise Men bring the baby Jesus?
    A. A baseball glove
    B. A ham
    C. A talking parrot that can sing "Silent Night"
    D. A New Testament

110. Which of the following is not a correct match of a man and his resolution?
    A. Martin of Tours—"I resolve to become a pacifist."
    B. Martin Luther—"I resolve to become a monk."
    C. Billy Sunday—"I resolve to give up my pro baseball career."
    D. Kenneth Hagin—"I resolve to accept my suffering."

SECTION 4

1. What three planets are the settings for C. S. Lewis's sci-fi novels, the Space Trilogy?
   A. Rigel V, Rigel VI, and Rigel VII
   B. Erewhemos, Erewhyna, and Erewhon
   C. Mars, Venus, and Earth
   D. Calormen, Archen, and Narnia

2. What are the significance of fish, reptile, mammal, Negro, Malaysian, American, and Mongolian?
   A. A nineteenth-century evolution text listed those as the stages of the fetal brain before it becomes British
   B. A nineteenth-century science text listed those as evolving species; all others were created
   C. In an infamous nineteenth-century sermon series, Charles Spurgeon listed those groups as "God's Seven Mistakes"
   D. A major nineteenth-century controversy centered on whether all of those groups were represented on the Ark

3. In the novel *In His Steps,* what four-word phrase do the committed disciples continually ask themselves?
   A. What would Jesus do?
   B. What would Paul say?
   C. What does Revelation mean?
   D. Am I having fun?

4. Twentieth-century Bible scholars debate whether Gospel writers, particularly Matthew, used the Hebrew technique of "midrash." What would be a contemporary example of midrash?
   A. The Living Bible
   B. Scripture choruses
   C. The dialogue in any religious Cecil B. deMille movie
   D. The chariot race in *Ben Hur*

5. What group of people did Roman Emperor Theodosius threaten in A.D. 380, declaring them "demented and insane"?
   A. Christians
   B. Non-Christians
   C. Monks
   D. His wife's relatives

6. What 1982 effort did *Newsweek* call "the most expensive Bible project in history"?
   A. The Sangtzee Edition of the Mandarin translation (for mainland China)
   B. The Wycliffe attempt to complete fifty-two translations in a single year
   C. The production of the New International Version
   D. The production of the New King James Version

7. What religious leader said the pattern of Christianity is "stoning prophets and erecting churches to their memory"?
   A. Gandhi
   B. Mohammed
   C. Martin Luther
   D. Anthony Campolo

8. When Zwingli became a Protestant, he determined to preach through the New Testament. How long did that project last?
   A. Just over six months (a book a week)
   B. Exactly five years (one chapter per week)
   C. Twelve years
   D. One week (he got so bogged down in the "begats" that he couldn't continue)

9. What unusual musical feature do the hymns "Awake! Awake!" and "Wonderful Grace of Jesus" have in common?
    A. In the chorus, the bass part sings the lead
    B. They are written for five parts rather than the usual four
    C. They both switch in the middle from 4/4 to 6/8 time
    D. They change keys between the verse and chorus

10. What poem or saying is traditionally the best-seller on gift items in Christian bookstores?
    A. "A Child's Ten Commandments"
    B. "Footprints"
    C. The Prayer of St. Francis of Assisi
    D. "Letter to a Friend"

11. What group of people were not allowed to teach at Oxford and Cambridge Universities until 1871?
    A. Catholics
    B. Baptists
    C. Atheists
    D. Anyone who was not Anglican

12. What religious item has (or had) forty-eight rubies, seventy-two sapphires, forty-five emeralds, and sixty-six pearls?
    A. The communion ware at the Crystal Cathedral
    B. The papal crown of Pope Boniface VIII
    C. Oral Roberts's bedroom suite
    D. The interior decorations of a cabin at a typical Christian camp

13. In *The City of God*, what did Augustine say would happen to all our fingernail trimmings and hair clippings when our bodies were resurrected?
    A. They will be attached back on and we will have extremely long hair and fingernails
    B. Nothing. They just disappear
    C. God turns them into other body elements (such as muscle or fat) and puts them where we need them
    D. The nail trimmings will go to women who want long nails; the hair will go to men who enter heaven bald

14. The movie *Shadowlands* centered on the marriage of what famous Christian couple?
    A. Jack (C. S.) and Joy Lewis
    B. Billy and Ruth Graham
    C. Martin and Katie Luther
    D. Peter and Catherine Marshall

15. What patriotic hymn has been sung with "Australia," "O Canada," and "O Africa" substituted in the chorus?
    A. "God of Our Fathers"
    B. "Battle Hymn of the Republic"
    C. "This Is My Country"
    D. "America the Beautiful"

16. Which of the following is most typical of Ann Kiemel Anderson's evangelism style?
    A. "Hi! I'm Ann, and I'm out to change my world. Care for a chocolate chip cookie"?
    B. "Turn or burn! Fly or fry! Holy Ghost or roast!"
    C. "If you give me thirty minutes, I can change your mind. If you give me sixty minutes, I can change your life"
    D. (Between sobs) "I'm sorry. Thinking of you without the Lord Jesus makes me cry"

17. Who at his death allegedly said, "Galilean, Thou hast conquered"?
    A. Voltaire
    B. Rousseau
    C. Julian the Apostate
    D. Charles Darwin

18. How old is the world's oldest religious stained glass artwork?
    A. 1,800 years old
    B. 1,500 years old
    C. 1,200 years old
    D. 900 years old

19. What verse of Scripture did Henry VIII use to justify his divorce from Catherine of Aragon, which led to the founding of the Anglican Church?
    A. "When a man hath taken a wife, and she find no favor in his eyes, let him write her a bill of divorcement"
    B. "If a man shall take his brother's wife, it is an unclean thing"
    C. "For this deed of the queen shall come abroad unto all women so that they shall despise their husbands"
    D. "Have ye forgotten the wickedness of your wives"?

20. What was Corrie ten Boom's honored nickname in Southeast Asia?
    A. Fountain of Wisdom
    B. Survivor
    C. Double-old Grandmother
    D. One Who Listens

21. Except for the first verse, "Jesus Loves Me" is a surprisingly unfamiliar song. Which of these phrases does not start one of the other three verses?
    A. "Jesus loves me, loves me still"
    B. "Jesus loves me, takes my hand"
    C. "Jesus loves me, He who died"
    D. "Jesus loves me, He will stay"

22. What is the meaning of "Maranatha," the word said at the end of many communion services in the early church?
    A. "Bittersweet" (referring to the taste of wine and the feeling of forgiveness)
    B. "Our Lord, come"
    C. "You are my brothers"
    D. "Have a nice day"

23. Why was the Crusade of 1203 called "The Crusade against Christians"?
    A. The Moslems were invading Europe to attack it
    B. Two cardinals wanted to assume the vacant papacy and raised "crusades" against each other
    C. When the Crusaders saw how rich Constantinople was, they attacked it instead of going on to Jerusalem
    D. On the way back from their defeat, the Crusaders in their anger ravaged the entire country of Bohemia

24. What occurs in a contemporary church during a "sharing time"?
    A. Members contribute furniture, appliances, clothing, etc., rather than money
    B. Everyone prays at the same time
    C. Individuals stand up and talk about their experiences with God during the previous week
    D. Members go to each other and ask forgiveness for sins they have committed against each other

25. Complete this Augustinian saying: "Our hearts are restless. . ."
    A. "and we wish they weren't"
    B. "but there is no rest"
    C. "till they rest in Him"
    D. "and our minds are fruitless"

26. To what extent did the famous Mount Athos monastery carry its prohibition against women?
    A. Any woman touching the mountain was whipped
    B. Any monk seeing a woman near the mountain was whipped
    C. The monks prayed daily for God to protect the monastery from women
    D. Female animals were forbidden on the mountain

27. What organization began asking Sunday school children for trick-or-treat money in 1950?
    A. The National Sunday School Board
    B. UNICEF
    C. The PLO
    D. The American Bible Society

28. What animal do the initial letters of "Jesus Christ, God's Son, Savior" spell in Greek?
    A. Lamb
    B. Lion
    C. Fish
    D. Goat

29. John Wycliffe was the first European to identify the pope with what biblical figure?
    A. Peter
    B. God
    C. Christ
    D. Antichrist

30. When homemaker Annie Hawks asked God to be with her during each of her household chores, what hymn did she write?
    A. "I Need Thee Every Hour"
    B. "Count Your Blessings"
    C. "Just As I Am"
    D. "Nothing but the Blood of Jesus"

31. After Martin Luther once confessed for six straight hours, why did he feel so bad a few minutes later?
    A. He remembered another sin
    B. He had made most of those sins up
    C. He found out his confessor was telling Luther's sins to the rest of the monastery
    D. He still didn't feel forgiven

32. When the pope claimed the power to release people from purgatory, what was Martin Luther's comment?
    A. "Then why doesn't he empty the place"?
    B. "He's putting me through purgatory every day; why won't he release me"?
    C. "His death will release more people from purgatory than anything else he can do"
    D. "I have the same power; I declared purgatory nonexistent"

33. What was Thomas Aquinas's nickname in seminary?
    A. Dumb Ox
    B. Boarhead
    C. Turkeyneck
    D. Proud Peacock

34. Why was an hourglass found on many eighteenth-century English pulpits?
    A. To keep sermons from lasting more than an hour
    B. To keep sermons from lasting less than an hour
    C. To symbolize the sands of life running out
    D. Parliament had passed a law against having clocks in church buildings

35. Chartres Cathedral, begun about 1140, was the first church built in what style?
    A. Early American
    B. Romanesque
    C. Gothic
    D. Doric

36. Which of the following is not a modern Christian writer?
    A. Keith Miller
    B. Charles Swindoll
    C. Marvin D. Hinten
    D. Arthur C. Clarke

37. For what are Don Marsh and John W. Peterson noted?
    A. Their Christmas and Easter cantatas
    B. Their religious Argus posters
    C. Their invention of "Faith-Promise" campaigns
    D. Their contributions founded Taylor University and Fuller Seminary, respectively

38. What was William Booth's official title?
    A. Ambassador to Ireland
    B. Doctor of Arts
    C. General of the Army
    D. Supreme Head of the Church

39. When the Roman Empire began to fall, what Christian refusal most inflamed the emperors?
    A. Christians wouldn't work on Sunday
    B. Christians wouldn't pray for the empire to survive
    C. Christian men wouldn't be soldiers
    D. Christian women wouldn't try to increase their childbearing to repopulate the empire

40. How many children did Susanna Wesley and her mother give birth to (combined)?
    A. Fourteen
    B. Twenty-four
    C. Thirty-four
    D. Forty-four

41. Which two of these songs can be sung to each other's tunes?
    A. "I Will Sing of My Redeemer"
    B. "I Will Sing the Wondrous Story"
    C. "Jesus Calls Us O'er the Tumult"
    D. "Jesus, Savior, Pilot Me"

42. Who described pain as God's "megaphone to rouse a deaf world"?
    A. Thomas à Kempis
    B. C. S. Lewis
    C. Philip Yancey
    D. Max Lucado

43. What is the most famous description of the Holy Roman Empire?
    A. "One country ruled by two kings"
    B. "The empire Jesus founded and was asked to abdicate from"
    C. "Neither holy, nor Roman, nor an empire"
    D. "A desert in the oasis of history"

44. The Montanists, a Christian offshoot in the early third century, were condemned for all of the following except what?
    A. Ecstatic utterances from the Holy Spirit
    B. Prophecy
    C. Healings
    D. Diets of radishes

45. How tall was "Jesus" when he allegedly appeared to Oral Roberts in 1981?
    A. 5 feet, 10 inches
    B. 6 feet, 3 inches
    C. 9 feet, 9 inches
    D. 900 feet

46. What character in Milton's *Paradise Regained* refers to common people as "a herd confused, a miscellaneous rabble"?
    A. Simon Peter
    B. Satan
    C. Simon the Pharisee
    D. Jesus

47. What contemporary Christian singer is known for his story songs, such as "Lazarus" and "Sunday's on the Way"?
    A. Steve Green
    B. Bryan Duncan
    C. David Meece
    D. Carman

48. What preacher's success could be seen, in his
    words, in "white channels left by tears on coal-
    blackened cheeks"?
    A. Walter Scott
    B. Charles Spurgeon
    C. George Whitefield
    D. G. Campbell Morgan

49. What work discusses 512 theological points,
    including whether an angel can sin?
    A. *Summa Theologica*
    B. *Institutes of the Christian Religion*
    C. *The Moody Encyclopedia of
       Christian Knowledge*
    D. The Bible

50. What unexpected breakthrough in Mormon evan-
    gelism occurred in 1980?
    A. The first president of the Church,
       Spencer Kimball, converted to
       Christianity
    B. A controversy over celestial mar-
       riage split the church and opened up
       many Mormons to Christianity
    C. The Mormon Church republished
       the original Book of Mormon
    D. The film *Wolves in Sheep's Clothing*
       was shown to huge crowds through-
       out Utah

51. At what sport did missionary Ida Scudder continue to trounce teenagers when she was in her sixties?
    A. Golf
    B. Tennis
    C. Chess
    D. Auto racing

52. In most medieval and Renaissance dialogues, what two parts of a person speak to each other?
    A. The heart and mind
    B. The eye and ear
    C. The tongue and mind
    D. The soul and body

53. What "Peanuts" character has the same name as a person in the New Testament?
    A. Charlie (Brown)
    B. Lucy
    C. Linus
    D. Schroeder

54. What is the Septuagint?
    A. The oldest translation of the Bible
    B. Greek for "the Sabbath"
    C. The papal ring that must be kissed by visiting religious leaders
    D. The council of A.D. 432 that approved the death penalty for women attending church without a veil

55. Complete this saying by Corrie ten Boom:
"There is no pit so deep—"
   A. "That the Light does not shine into it"
   B. "As the pit of self-'pit'y'"
   C. "As sin, or so steep"
   D. "That Jesus is not deeper still"

56. Which of the following was a religious television cartoon series?
   A. Transformers
   B. Kingdom Chums
   C. Masters of the Universe
   D. Care Bears

57. What was Paterson's Blasphemy Depot?
   A. A London station where trains were habitually late, causing cursing among the passengers
   B. England's leading atheist bookstore
   C. The nickname for the study library where Oxford critics took apart the Bible
   D. A London subway line that had blasphemous graffiti scribbled all over the walls

58. What was the unusual occupation of Timothy Dwight, composer of "I Love Thy Kingdom, Lord"?
    A. He was an indentured servant
    B. He was an anvil salesman
    C. He was president of Yale University
    D. He was vice-president of the United States

59. What explorer wrote in his logbook, "Your Highnesses decided to send me to the princes of India to consider the best means for their conversion"?
    A. Christopher Columbus
    B. John Cabot
    C. Ferdinand Magellan
    D. Vasco da Gama

60. Which of the following was not one of the general rules John Calvin set up for the citizens of Geneva, Switzerland to follow?
    A. A marriage couldn't be arranged between a woman of seventy and a man of twenty-five
    B. A woman couldn't say "rest in peace" over her husband's grave
    C. People couldn't sing songs that made fun of Calvin
    D. Bread had to be baked in the shape of a cross

61. Which of Pat and Shirley Boone's daughters describes her struggle with anorexia, including the use of up to sixty laxatives at a time, in the book *Starving for Attention*?
    A. Cherry
    B. Lindy
    C. Debby
    D. Laury

62. How many theses did Martin Luther nail up for discussion to the Wittenberg Door?
    A. Five
    B. Thirty-five
    C. Sixty-five
    D. Ninety-five

63. In 1974 the Vatican announced that the Jewish people should no longer be held responsible for what?
    A. The fall of man
    B. Their failure to convert
    C. The crucifixion
    D. Their wars with the Arabs

64. To what creature does Jonathan Edwards compare sinners in his famous sermon "Sinners in the Hands of an Angry God"?
    A. A slug
    B. A spider
    C. A roach
    D. A scorpion

65. What repeated punishment did Athanasius receive from his church because he believed in the Trinity?
    A. He was stoned three times
    B. He was whipped five times
    C. He was exiled seven times
    D. He was shaved nine times

66. Which of these hymn titles is not a direct quote from Scripture?
    A. "Holy, Holy, Holy"
    B. "I Know That My Redeemer Liveth"
    C. "I Know Whom I Have Believed"
    D. "O Master, Let Me Walk with Thee"

67. Which of the following is not a top-selling teen devotional by Lorraine Peterson?
    A. *If God Loves Me, Why Can't I Get My Locker Open?*
    B. *If Life Is a Bowl of Cherries, What Am I Doing in the Pits?*
    C. *Why Isn't God Giving Cash Prizes?*
    D. *Falling Off Cloud Nine and Other High Places*

68. British poet William Cowper tried to drown himself in the Thames River. But instead of drowning that night, he wrote the hymn "The Lord Moves in a Mysterious Way." Why?
    A. When he jumped off London Bridge, he landed on an empty pig shed floating down the river
    B. A passerby jumped into the water and saved him; it turned out to be Cowper's pastor
    C. A woman was also there to jump. Cowper talked her out of it, and the two of them got married
    D. The cab driver taking Cowper to the river got lost and dropped Cowper off at his own home

69. Which of the following is not an achievement of Jonathan Edwards?
    A. He won the first chess tournament ever held in the American colonies, and remained champion for nine years
    B. He learned Latin at age six
    C. He graduated as valedictorian of Yale at age seventeen
    D. He spent thirteen hours a day in sermon preparation

70. For which one of the following fires were Christians blamed?
    A. Rome, first century
    B. Constantinople, eleventh century
    C. London, seventeenth century
    D. Chicago, nineteenth century

71. What famous eighteenth-century artist drew "Sleeping Congregation," which made his statement about the sermons of the day?
    A. Raphael
    B. William Hogarth
    C. Sir Joshua Reynolds
    D. Dante Gabriel Rossetti

72. How is the German phrase "Ein Feste Burg" generally translated into English?
    A. The Celebrating City
    B. The Holy Red (Wine)
    C. A Mighty Fortress
    D. In Remembrance of Me

73. From which of the following theologians' names do we get an English word meaning "a stupid person; numskull"?
    A. Philip Melancthon
    B. Desiderio Erasmus
    C. Jakobus Arminius
    D. Duns Scotus

74. From what Bible story did the "Breeches Bible" get its name?
    A. Adam and Eve
    B. Cain and Abel
    C. Samson and Delilah
    D. David and Goliath

75. When the pope (referring to the Vatican's wealth) said to Dominic, "The church can no longer say, 'Silver and gold have I none,' " what was Dominic's reply?
    A. "Not to mention diamonds, and onyx, and rubies, and . . ."
    B. "Neither can it any longer say, 'Rise up and walk' "
    C. "Peter gave us the keys to the treasury"
    D. "Would His Holiness be interested in making a small loan?"

76. What famous object did Martin Luther throw at the devil?
    A. His left shoe
    B. A salt shaker
    C. His false teeth
    D. An ink pot

77. Under the French Revolution's "decimal weeks,"
    how often did a day of rest occur?
    A. One day in four (a hundred hours)
    B. One day in three (ten days a month)
    C. One day in ten
    D. Ten hours a day

78. Which of the following is outranked by the oth-
    ers in medieval angelology?
    A. Thrones
    B. Dominions
    C. Principalities
    D. Archangels

79. According to the doctrine of the Immaculate
    Conception, whose conception was supposed to
    be "immaculate"?
    A. Every Christian's
    B. Jesus'
    C. Mary's
    D. Adam's

80. According to the Didache, what did the early
    Christians wear when being baptized?
    A. Their usual clothes
    B. A white loincloth to symbolize purity
    C. A red veil, representing sin, which
       floated down the river as they were
       immersed
    D. Nothing—they were baptized nude

81. Which of the following, from the Seven Wonders of the Ancient World, is mentioned in the Bible?
    A. The Hanging Gardens of Babylon
    B. The Pyramids
    C. The Lighthouse of Pharos
    D. The Temple of Diana at Ephesus

82. In Michelangelo's Sistine Chapel painting, what two Biblical figures reach toward each other's fingers?
    A. Jesus and Mary
    B. Adam and Eve
    C. God and Adam
    D. Jesus and a leper

83. With what hymn are Billy Graham Crusades usually associated?
    A. "Make Me a Blessing"
    B. "O Why Not Tonight"?
    C. "Just As I Am"
    D. "Christian, Walk Carefully"

84. What act was punished by early Irish monks for being an indication of gluttony?
    A. Being overweight
    B. Cooking (rather than eating food raw)
    C. Vomiting
    D. Licking out the bowl

85. All of the following are true of author Elisabeth Elliot except which?
    A. Her first husband died of martyrdom
    B. Her second husband died of cancer
    C. She has served several years as a missionary in South American jungles
    D. Her pet mule, Bitsy, would bray whenever someone said, "John 3:16"

86. How many religious poems did Charles Wesley write?
    A. 8
    B. 89
    C. 898
    D. 8,989

87. Who was the first president to declare Thanksgiving a national holiday?
    A. George Washington
    B. Millard Fillmore
    C. Abraham Lincoln
    D. Grover Cleveland

88. When Constantine became Roman emperor in 323, approximately what percentage of the empire's population was Christian?
    A. Less than one percent
    B. Three percent
    C. Ten percent
    D. Forty percent

89. What famous psychologist explained belief in God as an extension of our father-love, failing to realize that his atheism could thus be traced to his dislike of his own father?
    A. Freud
    B. Adler
    C. Jung
    D. Maslow

90. Why did many church members boycott the Nestle's Corporation in the 1970s?
    A. Nestle's was the world's largest producer of infant formula
    B. Nestle's ran a contest in which the first prize was 666 candy bars
    C. Sun Myung Moon was named to the Nestle's board of directors
    D. Christian Against Acne (CAA) released a study showing chocolate more harmful than nicotine

91. Which of these birds is mentioned in the title of a famous gospel song?
    A. Starling
    B. Sparrow
    C. Raven
    D. Crow

92. Christian hermits in the Middle East lived on pillars, as much as six stories high, to separate themselves from the sinful world. How long did this "pillar hermit" fad last?
    A. Only six months. It never really got off the ground
    B. Sixty years
    C. 200 years
    D. 1,200 years

93. Why was an armed guard placed around the deathbed of Francis of Assisi?
    A. To get more relics, some churches had started cutting off body parts before the saints finished dying
    B. There was a prophecy that when Francis died, the Antichrist would take over his body and rule the world
    C. During the last few weeks of his life, the mild-mannered Francis became violently insane
    D. Since Francis loved animals so much, they were afraid he would pretend to be dead for the vultures

94. On what television show did ordained Southern Baptist minister Grady Nutt regularly appear?
    A. "Gilligan's Island" (as the professor)
    B. "Laugh-In" (as himself)
    C. "Hee-Haw" (as himself)
    D. "Green Acres" (as Sam Drucker)

95. If tradition is true, what was the chief difference in the crucifixions of Jesus and Peter?
    A. Peter was killed before being placed on the cross
    B. Peter was crucified upside-down
    C. Peter's clothes were left on
    D. Peter hung on the cross for three days

96. To humble the argumentative King Henry IV of Germany, Pope Gregory VII made Henry stand barefoot in the snow outside his (Gregory's) castle in the Alps. For how long?
    A. One hour
    B. Six hours
    C. All day
    D. Three days

97. Protestant Christianity grew quickly in Latin America in the mid-twentieth century (and still is growing). By what percentage did evangelical Christians increase from 1915 to 1960?
    A. 400 percent
    B. 40,000 percent
    C. 4,000,000 percent
    D. 400,000,000 percent

98. What restriction did Henry VIII place on oral
    Bible-reading in 1543?
    A. It could only be done in church
    B. It could only be done for the
       families of nobles
    C. It had to be the King James version
    D. It could only be from the New
       Testament

99. Clovis, king of the Franks, became a Christian
    about 500. A typical conversion of royalty in that
    period, it involved all of the following except
    which?
    A. Clovis said he'd become a Christian
       if God would help him win an im-
       portant battle
    B. He forced 3,000 of his soldiers to
       be baptized right away
    C. He continued to engage regularly
       in treachery and murder
    D. He took over all church lands and
       buildings within his territory

100. What group of people originally fought for the
     right to affirm in court rather than having to
     swear on a Bible?
     A. Quakers
     B. Mennonites
     C. Churches of Christ
     D. Atheists

101. What, according to Archbishop Ussher, began Sunday, October 23, 4004 B.C.?
    A. The world
    B. The Hebrew race
    C. The fall of mankind
    D. The Tower of Babel

102. A leading Christian heavy metal band was frequently attacked by Jimmy Swaggart, despite the fact that two band members were converted through his show. What was the band?
    A. Allies
    B. Petra
    C. Stryper
    D. Whiteheart

103. On Christmas Day, 1933, what did the Soviet government sell to the British government for half a million dollars?
    A. The oldest Protestant cathedral in Russia
    B. The world's oldest manuscript of the New Testament
    C. The Shroud of Turin
    D. The Bishop of Whitby, who had been captured while secretly encouraging Russian Christians

104. What translation, "faithfully and truly translated
     out of Douche and Latyn in to Englishe," was the
     first Bible printed in English?
     A. Bishops' Bible
     B. Geneva Bible
     C. Wycliffe's Bible
     D. Cranmer's Bible

105. Which of these ladies used her TV appearances
     on "Hee-Haw" as a springboard to a Southern
     gospel singing career?
     A. Minnie Pearl
     B. Cathy Baker
     C. Susan Ray
     D. Lulu Roman Smith

106. In what Christmas carol does one find the words
     "Veiled in flesh the Godhead see"?
     A. "It Came upon the Midnight Clear"
     B. "Rise Up, Shepherds, and Follow"
     C. "Hark, the Herald Angels Sing"
     D. "We Three Kings of Orient Are"

107. Which of the following is not symbolism used in
     medieval artwork?
     A. An owl stands for wisdom
     B. A lily stands for chastity
     C. A lamb stands for Christ
     D. Fire stands for zeal

108. How much were Union chaplains paid by the
     U. S. government during the Civil War?
     A. $10 a month
     B. $100 a month
     C. $1,000 a month
     D. Nothing. Their work was consid-
         ered to be a "ministry," so they
         were given only room and board

109. According to G. K. Chesterton, why does the
     Bible specify that we should love both our neigh-
     bors and our enemies?
     A. Because so often they are the same
         people
     B. Because we are so eager to look
         for loopholes
     C. Because our neighbors may be
         another Christian's enemies
     D. Because our enemies may be another
         Christian's neighbors

110. Three of the following are lines from contempo-
     rary Christian songs. Which one is a fake?

     A. "Give me your unconditional love,
         the kind of love I deserve." (Donna
         Summer)

     B. "He's a supernatural plowboy dressed
         up kinda strange." (Barry McGuire)

     C. "If your hair's too long, there's sin
         in your heart." (Ariel)

     D. "I found the Lord and I left off coke,
         it may sound funny but that's no
         joke." (Undercover)

SECTION 5

1. In a typical English city in 1820, less than one percent of seats in Anglican churches were what?
   A. Used on Sunday
   B. Free
   C. Wooden
   D. Clean, because of chewing gum stuck to the bottoms

2. To whom were Russian children taught to pray for daily bread in the 1920s?
   A. God
   B. Marx
   C. Lenin
   D. Themselves

3. What is a tessella?
   A. A hymn without a chorus
   B. The collar on a choir robe
   C. A small piece of glass used to make mosaics
   D. A Hebrew dance used by some religious groups that dance to the Lord

4. Who was the first church leader to suggest that the church should kill heretics?
   A. Martin Luther
   B. John Calvin
   C. Athanasius
   D. Augustine

5. In what decade were Christmas cards invented?
   A. The 1540s
   B. The 1640s
   C. The 1740s
   D. The 1840s

6. For what is Anglican bishop William Wilberforce most remembered?
   A. Two famous evangelists, Billy Sunday and Billy Graham, were both named after him
   B. He discovered that Piltdown Man, a so-called "Missing Link," was a hoax
   C. He led the fight to abolish England's slave trade
   D. He wrote and directed the first Christmas drama written in English

7. What is a "knee drill"?
   A. A warm-up activity used by the Fellowship of Christian Athletes
   B. Prayer, in the Salvation Army
   C. A piercing instrument of torture used by the Inquisition against heretics
   D. The motions to the children's religious song "Head and Shoulders, Knees and Toes"

8. What medical term comes from the Latin "I shall please," which was used at the start of Catholic vespers for the dead?
   A. Placebo
   B. Coagulate
   C. Euphoria
   D. Soporific

9. What childhood sin tortured Augustine more than any other?
   A. He took some pears from a neighbor's pear tree
   B. He lied to his parents about taking ten denarii
   C. He had frequent sexual daydreams
   D. He won a rhetoric contest in his grammar school with a speech stolen from the Roman orator Cicero

10. All of the following meteorological terms can be found in the titles of Christian hymns except which?
    A. Snow
    B. Fog
    C. Tempest
    D. Showers

11. What important Christian book did Hannah Whitall Smith write in the 1800s?
    A. *The Christian's Secret of a Happy Life*
    B. *The Abolition of Man*
    C. *The Late Great Planet Earth*
    D. *Hind's Feet on High Places*

12. Which of the following terms is not used in its language to describe a Nativity scene?
    A. French: Creche
    B. Italian: Presepio
    C. German: Krippe
    D. Spanish: Navidad

13. In what city is the world's largest Protestant church (numerically) located?
    A. Buenos Aires, Argentina
    B. Golden Grove, California
    C. Seoul, South Korea
    D. Dallas, Texas

14. After Constantine became a Christian supporter, he instituted all the following prison reforms except which?
    A. He allowed robbers to enlist in the army rather than go to prison
    B. He abolished crucifixion
    C. He halted the practice of branding criminals on the face so that they could be easily recognized
    D. He decreed that all prisoners must be allowed to see daylight once a day

15. C. S. Lewis became a believer in God in his room. But where did he become a believer in Christ?
    A. In the sidecar of a motorcycle on the way to visit a zoo
    B. Attached to a parachute, approximately 600 feet from the ground
    C. In the barber shop, while having his throat shaved
    D. At Owen Barfield's home, at the end of a game of Monopoly (British edition)

16. Which of the following is not a book by the great Chinese Christian leader Watchman Nee?
    A. *Prison to Praise*
    B. *The Normal Christian Life*
    C. *Sit, Walk, Stand*
    D. *The Good Confession*

17. What, in the ninth century, was an iconoclast?
    A. A person who said the Lord's Prayer backwards
    B. A person who broke religious statues
    C. A layman who tried to drink Communion wine
    D. A hermit who would have himself buried in sand up to his neck to keep himself from sinning

18. What Christmas carol has the same tune as the hymn, "Fling Out the Banner"?
    A. "Come, Thou Long-Expected Jesus"
    B. "What Child Is This"?
    C. "I Heard the Bells on Christmas Day"
    D. "While Shepherds Watched Their Flocks"

19. Speaking of Christmas carols, one carol is the only hymn in history to use the word "ornery" in one of its verses. What carol?
    A. "I Wonder As I Wander"
    B. "Lo, How a Rose E'er Blooming"
    C. "Rise Up, Shepherds"
    D. "Go, Tell It on the Mountain"

20. Oswald Chambers is known as the author of one of the most popular devotional books of all time. Name it.
    A. *Streams in the Desert*
    B. *God Calling*
    C. *My Utmost for His Highest*
    D. *Come Before Winter*

21. Advent begins on the Sunday nearest what date?
    A. Thanksgiving
    B. November 30
    C. December 1
    D. December 2

22. The "twelve days of Christmas" end on January 6, which is called Epiphany or "Twelfth Night." What is that date's traditional significance?
    A. The disappearance of the Star of Bethlehem
    B. The circumcision of Jesus
    C. The blessings of Anna and Simeon in the temple
    D. The visit of the Wise Men

23. Christmas celebrations have varied greatly. What law did the English Parliament pass in 1644 regarding Christmas celebrations?
    A. Each family was to spend as much on presents for the poor as for their family gifts
    B. Trees were not allowed; the candles used to decorate them had burned down too many homes
    C. People were required to attend church on both Christmas Eve and Christmas morning
    D. It was illegal to celebrate Christmas in any way at all

24. What title was Charlemagne given on Christmas Day, A.D. 800?
    A. King of France
    B. Holy Roman Emperor
    C. Bishop of Tours
    D. Cardinal

25. What Christmas carol has three echoes in each verse, including one word that is repeated seven times in a row?
    A. "How Great Our Joy!"
    B. "The Star Carol"
    C. "As with Gladness Men of Old"
    D. "The First Noel"

26. Whose table grace was this: "Some people have food, but no appetite; some people have an appetite, but no food. I have both. The Lord be praised!"?
    A. Martin Luther
    B. Oliver Cromwell
    C. George Washington
    D. Davy Crockett

27. In what book did William Booth compare English slums to Africa?
    A. *Life Among the Lowly*
    B. *Mill on the Floss*
    C. *In Darkest England*
    D. *The Curse of Cain*

28. Where did Susanna Wesley begin her preaching ministry?
    A. In the barn
    B. In the living room
    C. In the kitchen
    D. On the front porch

29. What minor Bible character is the hymn "Almost Persuaded" written about?
    A. Felix
    B. Festus
    C. Bartholomew
    D. Agrippa

30. What is the Holy Grail?
    A. The basin Jesus washed the apostles' feet from
    B. The bread plate used at the Last Supper
    C. The cup used at the Last Supper
    D. The spear plunged into Jesus' side

31. All of the following are true of Queen Isabella of Spain except which?
    A. She wanted Columbus to Christianize any natives he might find
    B. She and Ferdinand drove the Moslem forces out of Spain, where they had been for 800 years
    C. She had only one bath her entire life, that being on her wedding day
    D. She turned Spain into the leading tennis-playing country in Europe

32. Approximately how much time elapsed between the last major persecution of Christians by pagans and the first major persecution of pagans by Christians?
    A. 10 years
    B. 80 years
    C. 240 years
    D. 550 years

33. What singer was nicknamed "The Voice" by the Christian music industry?
    A. Amy Grant
    B. Sandi Patti
    C. Tammy Bakker
    D. Steve Green

34. What American colony was established as a refuge for persecuted Catholics?
    A. Georgia
    B. South Carolina
    C. North Carolina
    D. Maryland

35. Who did Luther angrily say "wishes to reverse the entire science of astronomy; but sacred scripture tells us that Joshua commanded the sun to stand still, not the earth"?
    A. Galileo
    B. Newton
    C. Copernicus
    D. Erasmus

36. The music to "Joyful, Joyful We Adore Thee" is taken from what symphony?
    A. Brahms's Third
    B. Bach's Fifth
    C. Berlioz's Seventh
    D. Beethoven's Ninth

37. Which of the following is not a book by Corrie ten Boom?
    A. *Morning and Evening*
    B. *Tramp for the Lord*
    C. *In My Father's House*
    D. *The Hiding Place*

38. According to the doctrine of purgatory, how do the souls feel that are located there?
    A. Happy
    B. Miserable
    C. Perplexed
    D. Relaxed

39. The two leading religions in the Roman Empire were Christianity and Mithraism. Mithraism celebrated December 25 as its major holy day. Why?
    A. That was the projected date for the world's end
    B. That was the date of Nero's conversion to Mithraism
    C. That was the date of the sun-god's resurrection
    D. That was the date of the sun-god's birth

40. What English women were told to leave their homes under Henry VIII, get married under Edward VI, leave their husbands under Mary I, and return to their husbands under Elizabeth I?
    A. Members of the royal court
    B. Quakers
    C. Female preachers
    D. Nuns

41. What vision led to the conversion of Constantine?
    A. A flaming cross
    B. A glowing halo
    C. A sea of blood
    D. A speaking whale

42. What type of religious artwork begins with webbing in a frame?
    A. Ribbed vaults
    B. Stained glass
    C. Plaster-of-Paris figurines
    D. Fresco

43. Whiteheart and The New Gaither Vocal Band were highly dissimilar groups. The first was a rock band; the second was a Southern Gospel quartet. Who sang for both groups?
    A. Larnelle Harris
    B. Matthew Ward
    C. Gary McSpadden
    D. Steve Green

44. What does the term "Holy Lance" mean?
    A. It is the mispronunciation of the term "Holy Lands" by religious Pennsylvania Dutch settlers
    B. It was Lancelot's jousting title in the days of King Arthur
    C. It was the spear plunged into Christ's side
    D. It was the spear used by the Templars in the Crusades

45. What is the second division of Dante's *Divine Comedy*?
    A. Earth
    B. Hell
    C. Purgatory
    D. Heaven

46. What is the Tetragrammaton?
    A. The Moslem monument captured by the First Crusade
    B. The sacred Hebrew name for God
    C. The papyrus fragment found in a pyramid in the late 1800s that enabled us to understand Aramaic grammar
    D. The record of the reign of Herod the Tetrarch, which mentions the slaughter of the infants at Jesus' birth

47. When an adult male serf died in medieval
    England, what did the priest take from his estate?
    A. His "best beast"
    B. His second-best beast
    C. His debts—they were paid by the
       church
    D. One-tenth of that year's harvest

48. Which of these is a religious "campfire song"?
    A. "Sha-Na-Na"
    B. "Sh-Boom"
    C. "Kum-Ba-Yah"
    D. "Ya-Ya"

49. Where did Bernard say all "murderers, rapists,
    adulterers, perjurers, and all other criminals"
    should go?
    A. To church
    B. To hell
    C. To monasteries
    D. To the Crusades

50. As of the early 1980s, what were the two kinds
    of churches one was most likely to find in a typi-
    cal American county?
    A. United Methodist and Catholic
    B. Catholic and Southern Baptist
    C. Southern Baptist and Assembly of God
    D. Assembly of God and Catholic

51. In eighteenth- and nineteenth-century books, one sometimes finds people called "free-thinkers." What do we call these people today?
    A. Agnostics
    B. Atheists
    C. Protestants
    D. Independent Christians (not denominational)

52. Which of the following is not a contemporary Christian music group?
    A. Journey
    B. Big Tent Revival
    C. 4 Him
    D. Glad

53. What ended on May 18, 1291?
    A. The Roman Empire
    B. Moslem control of Jerusalem
    C. Christian control of Jerusalem
    D. The final Crusade

54. What was the last book generally accepted as part of the New Testament?
    A. Hebrews
    B. James
    C. 2 Peter
    D. 3 John

55. Who, when he was dying, praised God for "Sister Death"?
    A. Bernard of Clairvaux
    B. Francis of Assisi
    C. John of the Cross
    D. Alvin of Avignon

56. What hymn were the passengers on the *Titanic* reportedly singing as it went down?
    A. "Now the Day Is Over"
    B. "Let the Lower Lights Be Burning"
    C. "When Peace Like a River"
    D. "Nearer, My God, to Thee"

57. What architect was buried in the London Cathedral he designed?
    A. Frank Lloyd Wright
    B. Frank B. Gilbreth
    C. Christopher Wren
    D. Louis Eiffel

58. What did President Reagan declare 1983 the year of?
    A. The church
    B. The family
    C. The Bible
    D. The unborn child

59. What couple, kept from marriage by (among other things) the fact that they were a monk and a nun, wrote the most romantic and heartbreaking series of love letters of the Middle Ages?
    A. Heloise and Abelard
    B. Abigail and Horace
    C. Teresa and Bartholomew
    D. Belinda and Thomas

60. What council did Pope John XXIII call that changed the Catholic mode of worship?
    A. Lateran I
    B. Lateran II
    C. Vatican I
    D. Vatican II

61. Who, during the German Peasants' War, encouraged rulers to "smite, slay, and stab" peasants like mad dogs?
    A. Menno Simons
    B. Philip Melancthon
    C. Desiderius Erasmus
    D. Martin Luther

62. The 1835 book *Life of Jesus* was the first complete biography of Christ to argue against what?
    A. Inerrancy
    B. Miracles
    C. The Trinity
    D. Jesus' being Jewish

63. What fictional work by Jonathan Swift tells about sons inheriting a coat from their father, but is really an allegory about Presbyterians, Lutherans, and Catholics?
    A. *Gulliver's Travels*
    B. "Tale of a Tub"
    C. "Coat of Many Colors"
    D. "The Inheritance"

64. Why did John Wesley allegedly get married on his knees?
    A. He had a sprained ankle
    B. He wanted to show how sacred the marriage vows were
    C. He wanted to show his humility for Molly
    D. Molly was extremely short, and he wanted them to balance

65. According to Augustine, the world will end when the total number of people saved equals what?
    A. The number of people killed in the Flood
    B. The number of sins committed by Adam
    C. The number of fallen angels
    D. The number of Jews since the time of Christ who have not believed

66. Which of the following is not a book by pastor and author Charles Swindoll?
    A. *Active Spirituality*
    B. *Conquering through Conflict*
    C. *Love Must Be Tough*
    D. *Dropping Your Guard*

67. Medieval wars were sometimes interrupted by the "Truce of God." What was that?
    A. Christian countries were not allowed to fight on Sundays or holy days
    B. If a roving friar could get a revival started in the armies, the soldiers would become pacifists and go home
    C. An earthquake during a war ended it. Quakes were seen as God's wrath (because of the one at the crucifixion)
    D. The pope's right to end one war per decade

68. What phrase in the Lord's Prayer causes the most confusion when large groups say it aloud together?
    A. Which art in heaven
    B. On earth as it is in heaven
    C. Forgive us our debts, as we forgive our debtors
    D. Thine is the kingdom, and the power, and the glory, forever

69. America's most famous Quaker poet wrote the quiet hymn, "Dear Lord and Father of Mankind." Who was he?
    A. Ralph Waldo Emerson
    B. John Greenleaf Whittier
    C. James Whitcomb Riley
    D. David Elton Trueblood

70. What twentieth-century Christian leader took his/her methods from a Hindu?
    A. Aimee Mcpherson
    B. Billy Sunday
    C. Dr. Martin Luther King, Jr.
    D. A. W. Tozer

71. Why did Tertullian argue in A.D. 200 that teenagers should not be baptized?
    A. They don't realize the depth of commitment required
    B. Jesus was not baptized until the age of thirty
    C. Teenagers sin a lot. A postponed baptism can forgive more sins
    D. According to legend, the youngest of the twelve disciples (John) was twenty-one when he was called

72. When John Calvin entered the University of Paris at the age of fourteen, what career accomplishment had he already achieved?
    A. He was fluent in Hebrew, Greek, Sanskrit, and Egyptian hieroglyphics
    B. He had written commentaries (in Latin) on twenty-one of the twenty-seven New Testament books
    C. He was not entering as a student; he had been hired as a professor
    D. He was already priest for about half a dozen churches

73. What brush with death made Martin Luther decide to become a monk?
    A. He was gored by a bull
    B. He was struck by lightning
    C. He became infected with the plague
    D. He was severely wounded in the Battle of Platenberg

74. What argument for the existence of God was advanced by William Paley in 1802?
    A. If there is a watch, there must be a watchmaker
    B. If there is an egg, there must be an eggbeater
    C. If there is an egg, there must be a hen
    D. If there is a digestive system, food must exist

75. Why did many people believe the early
    Christians to be cannibals?
    A. Before being converted, some of them
        actually had been cannibals
    B. They had secret burial services
    C. They took Communion
    D. Some of them drank blood to show
        their freedom from Mosaic law

76. Until 1828, Anglicans were the only people in
    England legally allowed to do what?
    A. Attend church
    B. Not attend church
    C. Hold public office
    D. Attempt to convert others to their faith

77. When Galileo was forced by the church to deny
    that the earth moves, what did he allegedly whis-
    per as he arose?
    A. "I had my fingers crossed"
    B. "God forgive me"
    C. "Let the future prove the right"
    D. "Nevertheless, it moves"

78. Joni Eareckson puts "PTL" at the bottom of her paintings and "Tada" at the bottom of her letters. "PTL" stands for "Praise the Lord." What does "Tada" stand for?

   A. "Totally alive, deeply aware"
   B. "Today alleluia, daily alleluia"
   C. "Touched and delivered—alleluia!"
   D. It doesn't stand for anything; it's her last name

79. In fourteenth-century England, what was unusual about the way the "kiss of peace" was handled in churches?

   A. There, for the first time, people switched the kiss to a handshake
   B. At one mass each quarter, the priest picked two known enemies to kiss each other before the congregation; if they refused, they were excommunicated
   C. Instead of kissing each other, people kissed a paddle and passed it on
   D. The kiss of peace was abandoned because in some churches people who did not want to be kissed slapped those who tried to kiss them

80. What is the best-known line of religious greeting cards for Valentine's Day and other holidays (individual, not boxed)?
    A. Morning Glory
    B. Evening Star
    C. Dayspring
    D. Nightlight

81. In 1509 a catalog was made of the relics in Martin Luther's church at Wittenberg, Germany. All of the following items from Jesus' birth were allegedly located there except which?
    A. Four pieces of Mary's girdle
    B. Some straw from the stable
    C. Some milk Jesus had spit up
    D. A piece of gold brought by the wise men

82. In what Shakespearian play does a king give up trying to pray with the remark, "My words fly up, my thoughts remain below/ Words without thoughts never to heaven go"?
    A. *Hamlet*
    B. *Henry IV, Part I*
    C. *Richard III*
    D. *King Lear*

83. George Whitefield was such a compelling evangelist that people said he could make converts simply by how he pronounced this word. What was the word?
    A. Calvary
    B. Golgotha
    C. Jerusalem
    D. Mesopotamia

84. What is a "chi-ro"?
    A. A very bad spelling of an Egyptian city
    B. A baptismal font in an Anglican church
    C. A Christian symbol formed from the first two letters in "Christ"
    D. An antiphonal medieval hymn, sung in Latin, now heard only in monasteries

85. What was Ignatius's comment about facing wild beasts in the coliseum where he would be martyred?
    A. "Better animal beasts than soldier beasts"
    B. "If God wills, the lions will lie before the Lamb"
    C. "I shall coax them to devour me promptly"
    D. "I shall not be facing the wildest beasts. They all sit in the coliseum bleachers!"

86. Which of the following Bible verses does not contain the name of a contemporary Christian music company?
    A. Then Jesus directed them to have all the people sit down in groups on the green grass (Mark 6:39)
    B. Hosanna to the Son of David! (Matthew 21:9)
    C. I have hidden your word in my heart that I might not sin against you (Psalm 119:11)
    D. Even the sparrow has found a home (Psalm 84:3)

87. What was unusual about the albums of contemporary Christian singer Keith Green?
    A. They were square instead of round
    B. He sold them for whatever people said they could afford
    C. Although he had three Number One singles, he never had a Number One album
    D. Because of his humility, his picture never appeared on an album cover until after his death

88. What is the primary claim to fame of William Barclay?
    A. He was the first NFL player to attribute victory to God at a Super Bowl postgame interview
    B. As a senator from Vermont, he founded the Congressional prayer breakfasts
    C. He wrote a well-known set of paper-back New Testament commentaries
    D. Starting from Manila, Philippines, he carried an eight-foot cross on his back around the world

89. In polls of church music leaders, "I Come to the Garden Alone" is consistently at or near the top in the "Worst Hymn" category. It is criticized for all the following except what?
    A. The beat of the melody sounds like a waltz
    B. In the last verse, Jesus asks the singer to go away from Him for no apparent reason
    C. The singer says no one else has ever had the happiness with Jesus that he has
    D. The second verse says that a Christian never has to undergo suffering as long as he loves Jesus

90. The fourth-century hermit Isidore used to cry
    when he ate. Why?
    A. He didn't like the food
    B. He felt it was an insult to our eternal
        nature to have to consume food as
        animals do
    C. He kept trying to go forty days without
        eating to imitate Jesus, but he never
        could achieve it
    D. He ate onions with every meal so he
        could shed genuine tears over his sins

91. When forty Roman soldiers in fourth-century
    Asia Minor became Christians, how were they
    martyred, and with what temptation to give in?
    A. They were drowned in only seven feet
        of water; they were told that by walk-
        ing forward, they could reject Christ
        and save themselves
    B. They were killed by spears, but shields
        were set up to protect them; they were
        told they could dodge behind a shield
        to reject Christ
    C. They were starved to death, with food
        placed at the hut doorway for anyone
        who would reject Christ
    D. They were placed naked on a frozen
        lake to freeze to death, with fires on
        the shore for anyone who would reject
        Christ

92. What is the difference between monks and friars?
    A. Monks live in rural areas, friars in cities
    B. Friars are required to perform manual labor, but not monks
    C. Monks withdraw from the world; friars live out among society
    D. Friar is a higher rank; only about fifteen percent of monks ever achieve it

93. "Onward Christian Soldiers" was first written as a march for children bearing crosses, but the cross-bearing part didn't work out. So what was the original ending?
    A. With the cross of Jesus, which we have no more
    B. With the cross of Jesus; buy one at the store
    C. With the cross of Jesus, dragging on the floor
    D. With the cross of Jesus, left behind the door

94. In the phrase "extreme unction," what does "unction" mean?
    A. Death
    B. Release
    C. Anointing
    D. Salvation

95. The two up-and-coming religions in the Roman
    Empire were Christianity and Mithraism, which
    both initiated converts by baptism. What liquid
    was used for Mithraic baptisms?
    A. Cold goat milk
    B. Lukewarm camel urine
    C. Warm wine
    D. Hot bull blood

96. Which of the following is not a character in
    Corrie ten Boom's *The Hiding Place?*
    A. Betsie
    B. Norman
    C. Willem
    D. Opa

97. For what Christian book is this the opening line:
    "There was a boy named Eustace Clarence
    Scrubb, and he almost deserved it"?
    A. *The Voyage of the Dawn Treader*
    B. *Born Again*
    C. *The Lord of the Rings*
    D. *Heaven Came Down*

98. How is church music sung if it is done "a cappella"?
    A. Off-key
    B. As a round
    C. Without instruments
    D. With each verse sung in a higher key

99. Approximately how many people went off on the First Crusade?
    A. 5,000
    B. 50,000
    C. 500,000
    D. 5,000,000

100. What preacher included these lines in his book *Country Rhymes for Children*: "An egg is not a chicken, by falling from a hen/Nor is a man a Christian, till he is born again"?
    A. John Bunyan
    B. John Wesley
    C. George Whitefield
    D. Charles Spurgeon

101. What does the "C. S." in C. S. Lewis stand for?
    A. Charles Stanley
    B. Clive Staples
    C. Chase Samuel
    D. Clifton Spurlock

102. Given his given names (see above), it is no wonder that at the age of four Lewis changed his name. What name did he go by for the rest of his life?
    A. Jack
    B. Matt
    C. Luke
    D. Phil

103. Besides C. S. Lewis and President Kennedy, what other writer died on November 22, 1963?
    A. Aldous Huxley
    B. George Bernard Shaw
    C. T. S. Eliot
    D. W. H. Auden

104. By curious coincidence, C. S. Lewis gave a title to one of his books that contained the name of his future wife, though at the time he had never met her. What was the book title?
    A. *Surprised by Joy*
    B. *Blessed with Peace*
    C. *Covered with Grace*
    D. *Surrounded by Hope*

105. What Narnian creature talks like this: "I doubt we'll catch any fish. If we do, they'll be too small to cook. But that's all right, because we'd just burn them, anyway"?
    A. A faun
    B. A talking horse
    C. A marshwiggle
    D. A dufflepud

106. Which of the Narnian Chronicles pictures baptism as turning a dragon into a boy?
    A. *The Lion, the Witch, and the Wardrobe*
    B. *The Voyage of the Dawn Treader*
    C. *The Horse and His Boy*
    D. *The Magician's Nephew*

107. In what year was the first Christmas card printed?
    A. 1543
    B. 1643
    C. 1743
    D. 1843

108. In A.D. 339 Martin of Tours made a comment about serving in the army that epitomizes Christian belief and practice in the first three centuries. What did he say?
    A. "I am Christ's soldier; I am not allowed to fight"
    B. "When I see a brother being harmed, brotherly love impels me to protect him"
    C. "Affairs of state are nothing to me; but for the honor of Christ I must take up arms against heretics"
    D. "The one who prays serves God, and the one who battles serves his fellow-man. We need both servants"

109. Hitler killed about 6,000,000 Jews. What fraction of the world's Jews was this?
    A. One-half
    B. One-third
    C. One-fifth
    D. One-eighth

110. In what period was Codex Sinaiticus, the oldest complete New Testament manuscript, copied?
    A. Around 100–150
    B. Around 200–250
    C. Around 300–350
    D. Around 400–450

SECTION 6

1. In what American magazine did C. S. Lewis's last article, "We Have No Right to Happiness," appear?
   A. *Ladies Home Journal*
   B. *Life*
   C. *Reader's Digest*
   D. *Saturday Evening Post*

2. Raymund of Pennafort, twelfth-century General of the Dominican order, was the first person in history to set sixty-five as a retirement age—in this case, for Dominican leaders. How did he arrive at that figure?
   A. He was sixty-five and wanted to retire
   B. If, according to the Bible, a standard maximum life span was threescore and ten, Raymund thought people deserved five years simply for worship
   C. Dominican friars had asked him to set a retirement age, so he set one so high he thought hardly anybody would reach it
   D. Seven and four were considered holy numbers, so Raymund squared them and added the squares together

3. Where is the world's oldest church building located?
   A. New Haven, Connecticut
   B. Antioch, Syria
   C. Istanbul, Turkey
   D. Alexandria, Egypt

4. Which of these was an issue causing the Roman Catholic and Greek Orthodox churches to separate in 1054?
   A. Should a monk wear a hair shirt?
   B. Should a friar wear shoes?
   C. Should a priest wear a beard?
   D. Should a bishop wear a head covering?

5. What flower is used as a mnemonic device by seminary students to remember the five points of Calvinism?
   A. Pansy
   B. Tulip
   C. Lilac
   D. Aster

6. What famous theologian turned away from theology toward the end of his life, declaring, "All my books are worthless"?
   A. Tertullian
   B. Origen
   C. Jerome
   D. Thomas Aquinas

7. The most prolific hymn writer in history, Fanny
Crosby, managed not to be bitter about her blind-
ness. What childhood event caused her to
become blind?
   A. She had a bad case of scarlet fever
   B. She stared at the sun during an eclipse
   C. A doctor prescribed mustard for her
      eyes during a cold
   D. She was abused by her father, who had
      wanted a son

8. Approximately when does the first mention of
infant sprinkling occur in the writings of the
church fathers?
   A. 90
   B. 190
   C. 290
   D. 390

9. April 23 is a significant day in British church his-
tory. All of the following happened on that day
except which?
   A. Thomas à Becket was born
   B. C. S. Lewis got married
   C. William Shakespeare died
   D. It's the saint day for St. George (the
      patron saint of England)

10. At the end of the Revolutionary War, approximately what percentage of Americans were church members?
    A. 5–10 percent
    B. 25–30 percent
    C. 45–50 percent
    D. 65–70 percent

11. What is the apparent origin of the word "teetotaler," referring in the early twentieth century to people who abstained from alcohol?
    A. Unlike some Christians, who abstained from hard liquor, they practiced "total" abstinence, including from beer and wine
    B. They claimed that people who drank did not practice the "total" gospel
    C. They refused to join country clubs, because most of those clubs had a bar called "The Nineteenth Tee"
    D. They got "teed off" (a slang phrase meaning "angry") with Christians who drank

12. Faith, hope, love, wisdom, courage, self-control. Which of the traditional Seven Cardinal Virtues is missing?
    A. Patience
    B. Justice
    C. Humility
    D. Honesty

13. If one is a church worker and not a hospital patient, what do the letters "IV" stand for?
   A. Jesus Victor
   B. I'm valuable
   C. Immaculate Virgin
   D. Inter-Varsity

14. The chorus of "Now I Belong to Jesus" is much more familiar than the verses. Which of the following is not the beginning of a verse from that hymn?
   A. "Joy floods my soul for Jesus has saved me"
   B. "Now I accept the love that He offers"
   C. "Jesus my Lord will love me forever"
   D. "Once I was lost in sin's degradation"

15. With what building is Robert Schuller most closely associated?
   A. The Chiming Church
   B. The Crystal Cathedral
   C. The Hall of Holiness
   D. Self-Esteem Sanctuary

16. When a young man in John Calvin's Geneva struck his parents, how did the city fathers respond?
   A. They asked him to apologize
   B. They required him to read the Old Testament seven times
   C. They had him flogged
   D. They had him beheaded

17. What kind of artwork, often religious, primarily uses pieces of glass from pinhead size to fingernail size?
    A. Origami
    B. Patriarchon
    C. Mosaic
    D. Iconography

18. Who or what is a "vulgate"?
    A. The obscene password of the Vulgarii, an influential second-century cult
    B. He was the last Roman emperor to worship the pagan gods
    C. The gate outside which Christian bodies were left in times of persecution (from "vulture gate")
    D. The Latin translation of the Bible used throughout the Middle Ages

19. Whose 6,500 hymns include some that seem today rather morbid, such as "Ah, lovely appearance of death!/ No sight upon earth is so fair/ Not all the gay pageants that breathe/ Can with a dead body compare"?
    A. Isaac Watts
    B. Charles Wesley
    C. Emily Dickinson
    D. Keith Green

20. Dunstan, Archbishop of Canterbury, became famous for his power against the devil. What tool did he allegedly use on Satan's nose?
    A. He pinched it with a pair of pliers
    B. He hit it with a hammer
    C. He scratched it with a rasp
    D. He bored it with an awl

21. Who wrote to her sister, "We shall have the right to speak because we can tell from our experience that His light is more powerful than the deepest darkness"?
    A. Harriet Beecher Stowe
    B. Susan B. Anthony
    C. Elizabeth Cady Stanton
    D. Betsie ten Boom

22. What was Carry Nation's favorite implement for smashing saloon furniture and bottles?
    A. A hatchet
    B. A sledgehammer
    C. A baseball bat
    D. A Bible

23. Many Catholics accused Erasmus of starting the Reformation because of his coming out with the New Testament in Greek. How did Erasmus respond?
    A. "Paul and John produced Greek before I did; blame them"
    B. "I don't understand this Reformation; it's Greek to me"
    C. "I laid a hen egg, but Luther hatched it into a rooster"
    D. "I gave men a lamp for their feet; Luther pushed it into their eyes so that they can't see the path"

24. Saints Anthony and Hilarion, two of the first Christian hermits, celebrated Easter by doing something they did not do any other day of the year. What?
    A. They took a bath
    B. They combed their hair
    C. They trimmed their nails
    D. They ate meat

25. Traditionally, monks have been required to make three vows. Which of the following is not one of those vows?
    A. Obedience
    B. Helpfulness
    C. Chastity
    D. Poverty

26. What is the correct listing of these three groups from largest to smallest (worldwide adherents)?
    A. Catholic, Protestant, Orthodox
    B. Catholic, Orthodox, Protestant
    C. Orthodox, Catholic, Protestant
    D. Protestant, Catholic, Orthodox

27. What member of the Blackwood Brothers and the Stamps Quartet was (deservedly) known as "The Lowest Bass Singer in the World"?
    A. James Blackwood
    B. Cecil Blackwood
    C. LaVerne Tripp
    D. J. D. Sumner

28. Augustine's mother Monica was raised in a very strict manner regarding wine and other alcoholic beverages. What was the strictest rule she and her sisters had to follow?
    A. They couldn't drink wine even at meals
    B. They couldn't drink water between meals
    C. They weren't allowed to see grapes
    D. Monica's sister wasn't allowed the customary wine (as anesthetic) before her tonsillectomy

29. After the Bible was divided into chapters, how many years passed before it was divided into verses?
    A. None—it was divided into verses five months later
    B. Ten
    C. 100
    D. 300

30. What John Donne poem title was used as the title of a John Gunther novel?
    A. "Death, Be Not Proud"
    B. "At the Round Earth's Imagined Corners"
    C. "Batter My Heart, Three-Personed God"
    D. "I Am a Little World Made Cunningly"

31. When the Greek Orthodox Church left the Roman Catholic Church, what was Pope Leo IX's reaction?
    A. "I hope they'll be very happy"
    B. "Let them be forever damned. Amen, amen, amen"
    C. "The Lord promises vengeance. We shall be His instruments"
    D. "The body of our Lord remained whole on the cross. Now, a thousand years later, it is torn"

32. Which of these song titles was first spoken by God to Moses?
    A. "The Lord Bless You and Keep You"
    B. "If My People"
    C. "How Firm a Foundation"
    D. "Cast Thy Burden upon the Lord"

33. Aside from geographical considerations, why do several nondenominational churches in the U.S. today have a tree and a body of water in their names?
    A. They want to present themselves as "a tree planted by the waters"
    B. They want to be associated with living water, and a tree sounds nice with that
    C. They want to present themselves as strong and flexible at the same time
    D. They have been influenced by the success of Willow Creek Church in Chicago

34. A colleague of mine said her husband preaches at a friend's church. What denomination is the church? (This is a trick question, but solvable using this information.)
    A. Free Will Baptist
    B. Quaker
    C. Presbyterian Church of America
    D. Nazarene

35. What are the two major branches of the Orthodox Church?
    A. Greek and Russian
    B. Roman and Neo
    C. Greek and Roman
    D. Russian and Roman

36. Which of the following was not a rule set up by John Calvin for "drinking places" (he closed the traditional taverns) in Geneva, Switzerland?
    A. The drinking limit was three beers or two glasses of wine
    B. Each drinking place had to have a Bible prominently displayed
    C. Drinkers were supposed to say grace before and after every drink
    D. Customers had a one-hour limit on card games

37. In 1980 the then fourth-ranked handball player in the United States, Terry Muck, began editing a religious journal. Which one?
    A. *Sojourners*
    B. *Discipleship Journal*
    C. *Leadership*
    D. *Christian Standard*

38. Augustine began reading Paul's epistles (which led to his conversion) because he heard a child chanting in a singsong voice. What were the child's words?
    A. "Take up and read"
    B. "Pay Paul"
    C. "It's in the letters"
    D. "Taste the words"

39. In "Beneath the Cross of Jesus," there are "two wonders I confess." What are they?
    A. Christ's body and Christ's blood
    B. God's justice and Christ's intercession
    C. Christ's suffering and Christ's mercy
    D. Christ's love and my unworthiness

40. In the fourth and fifth centuries, when people asked for baptism, how long were they generally required to wait?
    A. They were baptized the same day
    B. Till the following Sunday
    C. Till the next Easter
    D. About three years

41. In Bill and Gloria Gaither's chorus "Jesus, We Just Want to Thank You," what is Jesus thanked for?
    A. For saving our souls
    B. For loving us
    C. For answering prayer
    D. For being so good

42. When Christianity became established as the Roman religion in the fourth century, how long did a typical church service last?
    A. 3 hours
    B. 6 hours
    C. 9 hours
    D. 1 hour, 10:30–11:30 A.M.

43. Woodrow Kroll is teacher for what radio ministry?
    A. "Back to the Bible"
    B. "Thru the Bible"
    C. "A Word with You"
    D. "Focus on the Family"

44. What is the address of Doug Marlette's famous cartoon preacher Will B. Dunn?
    A. Overpass, Oklahoma
    B. Bypass, Georgia
    C. Side Road, South Dakota
    D. Wide Spot, Wyoming

45. The Tim Stafford column in *Campus Life* magazine answers questions on what topic?
    A. Christian views on sex
    B. Religious trivia
    C. Emotional difficulties
    D. Biblical interpretation

46. What sort of institution did Vincent de Paul, founder of the Daughters of Charity, most help to improve?
    A. Schools
    B. Hospitals
    C. Hotels
    D. Convents

47. Book trilogies are rare and movie trilogies rarer, but a record trilogy is virtually unheard of. What singer did an acclaimed album trilogy on the life of Christ?
    A. Steve Green
    B. Carman
    C. Larnelle Harris
    D. Michael Card

48. Augustus Toplady thought of the words to "Rock of Ages" while using a rock as shelter from a storm, but he had no paper. What did he find on the ground to write the words on?
    A. A piece of white elm bark
    B. His feet
    C. A six of diamonds playing card
    D. A page from Gibbon's *Decline and Fall of the Roman Empire* that argued against miracles

49. The Council of 1512 ordered priests not to attend the weddings of whom?
    A. People who had been excommunicated
    B. Protestants
    C. Former priests
    D. Their illegitimate sons and daughters

50. In Dante's *Inferno,* who are held by Satan in the deepest pit?
    A. Cain, Ahab, and Judas
    B. Judas, Nero, and Pope Innocent III
    C. Judas, Cassius, and Brutus
    D. Cain, Moloch, and Judas

51. What version of the Bible became the surprise runaway bestseller of the mid-1960s?
    A. King James
    B. New American Standard
    C. Living
    D. New International

52. What did Cardinal Hugo de Sancto Caro do to the Bible in A.D. 1250?
    A. Ripped it to shreds, declaring that it only misled people, anyway
    B. Did the first translation of it into an African language
    C. Divided it into chapters
    D. Banned its use in upper Italy

53. In order to hide their secret from the government, how did the ten Booms refer to the Jews hiding in their home during WWII?
    A. Puppies
    B. Valuables
    C. Clocks and watches
    D. Pots and pans

54. The author of what hymn described himself as "John Newton, clerk, once an infidel and libertine"?
    A. "To God Be the Glory"
    B. "Just As I Am"
    C. "Pass Me Not"
    D. "Amazing Grace"

55. Which of the following articles of clothing is not found in the lyrics of any standard Christian hymn?
    A. Tie
    B. Shirt
    C. Pants
    D. Robe

56. Early Christians sometimes met in catacombs. What are catacombs?
    A. Cemeteries
    B. Coliseum bleachers
    C. Bath houses
    D. Libraries

57. The remarkably brilliant John Wesley could have been successful in numerous fields. Which of the following did he *not* write a book about?
    A. Housekeeping
    B. Medicine
    C. Electricity
    D. Theology

58. What type of literary work did Augustine produce that appears to be the first of its kind in history?
    A. Bound volume of sermons
    B. A Petrarchan sonnet
    C. Interior autobiography
    D. Complete set of New Testament commentaries

59. Aksepsimas, strangest of all the ascetics, went without speaking for sixty years and had the usual aversion to personal hygiene. A shepherd once threw rocks at Aksepsimas. Why?
    A. His body odor was so bad it stampeded the sheep
    B. Aksepsimas thought the ultimate in self-denial would be to endure a stoning, so he requested one
    C. While the shepherd was bathing in a river, Aksepsimas burned his clothes to express disapproval
    D. Aksepsimas was so shaggy the shepherd mistook him for a wolf

60. Christian musician Don Francisco is perhaps best know for which song?
    A. "My Tribute"
    B. "Praise the Lord"
    C. "He's Alive!"
    D. "El Shaddai"

61. Complete this Peter Marshall quote: "Today's Christians are too often like deep-sea divers. . .
    A. . . . looking for oyster shells instead of the Pearl of Great Price"
    B. . . . looking at the oxygen hose and saying, 'I wonder what this is for?'"
    C. . . . with helmets on backwards, wondering where all the pearls disappeared to"
    D. . . . marching bravely forth to pull plugs out of bathtubs"

62. The worship of Mary began to take shape in the third through fifth centuries. All of the following practices arose at that time except which?
    A. The belief that Mary never died, but went straight to heaven (Assumption of the Virgin)
    B. Use of the term "The Mother of God"
    C. The belief that Mary never sinned
    D. The belief that Mary never had intercourse, even after the birth of Jesus

63. Macarius the Elder was one of the most respected ascetics of the fourth and fifth centuries. He disciplined his body by only eating once a week and by what unusual sleeping habit?
    A. He also slept only once a week
    B. He slept standing up
    C. He would sleep only on sharp rocks
    D. He slept with his eyes open (in an effort to obey literally the command to "watch")

64. What songwriting team wrote "Gentle Shepherd," "Let's Just Praise the Lord," "Because He Lives," and "The Family of God"?
    A. Bill and Gloria Gaither
    B. John W. and Mary Peterson
    C. Michael Ward and Anne Herring
    D. Richard Rodgers and Oscar Hammerstein

65. The most important Bible translating in the church's first thousand years was done by Jerome. Into which language did he translate the Bible?
    A. Anglo-Saxon
    B. Persian
    C. Old Norse
    D. Latin

66. What contemporary Christian singer served as mother for her brother and sister, who are also contemporary Christian singers?
    A. Nancy Honeytree
    B. Twila Paris
    C. Anne Herring
    D. Wendy Talbot

67. According to Catholic doctrine, the pope is infallible when speaking *ex cathedra*. What, originally, was a cathedra?
    A. The chair a bishop sat in to decide church cases
    B. The scepter a bishop waved to call for silence
    C. The room where an emperor set the seal on new laws
    D. The designated spokesman for a church council

68. "God creates out of nothing. Therefore, until a man is nothing, God can make nothing out of him." Who said that?
    A. Albert Einstein
    B. C. S. Lewis
    C. Savonarola
    D. Martin Luther

69. According to early twentieth-century evangelist Billy Sunday, going to church doesn't make you a Christian any more than—
    A. going to the grocery store makes you a turnip
    B. going to the dentist makes you a set of dentures
    C. going to a garage makes you an automobile
    D. going to a dance makes you a corsage

70. According to Reinhold Neibuhr, the job of a preacher is to—
    A. enlighten the puzzled and puzzle the enlightened
    B. comfort the disturbed and disturb the comfortable
    C. puff up the deflated and deflate the puffed up
    D. relax the uptight and tighten up the lax

71. What did Henry II do to show he was sorry for getting the Archbishop of Canterbury, Thomas a Becket, killed?
    A. He donated land for monasteries in six counties
    B. He killed himself
    C. He read the entire Bible clear through (for the first time)
    D. He had monks whip him

72. Many of the children who embarked on the "Children's Crusade" halted in Italy. What happened to the ones who actually made it to the sea?
    A. They tried to walk through it, believing it would part for them, and over 800 children drowned
    B. They received a "vision" to return home
    C. Christian shipowners took them to northern Africa, where most of the children became Moslem
    D. Christian shipowners sold most of them to the Moslems as slaves

73. Which of the following elementary school action series is produced by a Christian publisher?
    A. Sugar Creek Gang
    B. Bobbsey Twins
    C. Hardy Boys
    D. Trixie Belden

74. Who said the following: "My father was a Methodist and believed in the laying on of hands, and believe me, he really laid them on!"?
    A. C. S. Lewis
    B. J. R. R. Tolkien
    C. A. W. Tozer
    D. Billy Graham

75. Complete Walter Horton's intriguing comment on church types: "It is easier to tame a fanatic than—
    A. to marry one"
    B. to understand one"
    C. to wake up the sleepy"
    D. to put life into a corpse"

76. One of the most feared religious weapons in the medieval world was the interdict. What is an interdict?
    A. The bishops' right to declare priests heretics on the basis of a single sermon
    B. The refusal of Communion or other sacraments to everyone in a certain territory
    C. Punishing a person caught giving less than ten percent to the church by forcing him to give fifty percent for the next seven years
    D. Burning at the stake

77. What kind of Christian organization is "AIA"?
    A. A basketball team
    B. A campus organization
    C. A trio
    D. A pro-life group

78. How far back does the oldest church building go?
    A. A.D. 232
    B. A.D. 332
    C. A.D. 432
    D. A.D. 532

79. Joni Eareckson Tada, despite her quadriplegia, does all of the following except which?
    A. Drive a van
    B. Play wheelchair basketball
    C. Paint
    D. Head a Christian organization

80. The sixteenth-century British ship *Jesus* was the largest of its kind, twice as big as the *Nina, Pinta,* and *Santa Maria* combined. What was the *Jesus* used for?
    A. It carried Bibles to Oriental countries for mission work
    B. It transported religious dissenters to America
    C. It was a sort of luxurious summer home for Pope Benedict IV
    D. It transported slaves from Africa

81. Which of the following is a C. S. Lewis quote?
    A. "Everyone says forgiveness is a lovely idea, until they have something to forgive"
    B. "Domestic happiness depends upon the ability to overlook what's under-cooked"
    C. "God helps those that help themselves"
    D. "To strive, to seek, to find, and not to yield"

82. What article of clothing was the trademark of Christian poet Helen Steiner Rice?
    A. Shoes with bows
    B. Long wool skirts
    C. A ring on every finger
    D. Floppy hats

83. The author of *The Alchemy of the Heart* and *Wide My World, Narrow My Bed* is the sister of a famous male Christian writer. Name this sister.
    A. Luci Swindoll
    B. Danae Dobson
    C. Carol Schuller
    D. Ruth Graham

84. One of the traditional "Seven Works of Mercy" is clothing the naked. Which of the following pairs of works are not on that list?
    A. Feeding the hungry and giving water to the thirsty
    B. Converting the lost and avenging the downtrodden
    C. Visiting the sick and housing the homeless
    D. Ransoming captives and burying the dead

85. What name is found in the hymn "This Is My Father's World"?
    A. Chris
    B. Holly
    C. Carol
    D. Sandy

86. Ignatius Loyola, founder of the Jesuits, set up a "five-finger plan" for self-examination. Steps 1–4 are: Give thanks, Ask for light, Look at yourself, and Be sorry. What's Step 5?
    A. Give thanks again
    B. Ask forgiveness
    C. Do something constructive
    D. Remember sins no more

87. Who wrote letters to Karen and Philip?
    A. Anyone who missed them
    B. C. S. Lewis
    C. J. Vernon McGee
    D. Charlie Shedd

88. What is the longest book of the New Testament?
    A. Matthew
    B. Luke
    C. John
    D. Acts

89. A few centuries ago, the word "frame" meant "state of mind." Among some groups, having a positive frame determined whether one was saved. What hymn combats this notion?
    A. "My Hope Is Built on Nothing Less"
    B. " 'Tis So Sweet to Trust in Jesus"
    C. "My Faith Looks up to Thee"
    D. "The Haven of Rest"

90. Only one of the following quotes is from the Bible. Which one?
    A. "The Lord helps those that help themselves"
    B. "Cleanliness is next to godliness"
    C. "Neither a borrower nor a lender be"
    D. "Out of the mouths of babes"

91. "If you were to live a thousand years, you could not undo the mischief you have done." Who wrote that as a final letter to whom?
    A. Martin Luther to Tetzel regarding indulgences
    B. Erasmus to Martin Luther regarding the Reformation
    C. John Wesley to his wife regarding their unhappy marriage
    D. Tammie Faye Bakker to Jim Bakker regarding his affair

92. What is "vellum"?
    A. The Latin word for committed sin (as opposed to original sin)
    B. Calfskin parchment that Scripture was sometimes written on
    C. The opening word of High Mass (before Vatican II)
    D. It was the sealed envelope which carried the pope's orders to the cardinals in medieval times

93. In Dante's *Inferno,* what sinners are punished by being completely submerged in a filthy marsh for eternity, with the rising bubbles the only evidence of their presence?
    A. Sulkers
    B. Backbiters
    C. Gluttons
    D. Traitors

94. Corrie ten Boom said we should throw our sins into the middle of the sea and put up a sign over them. What should the sign say?
    A. "Sins buried here"
    B. "Look out below!"
    C. "Nuclear waste"
    D. "No fishing"

95. Who said, "I want to be the white man's brother, not his brother-in-law"?
    A. Jesse Jackson
    B. Martin Luther King, Jr.
    C. Stokely Carmichael
    D. Bill Cosby

96. Due to a misprint, what "commandment" appeared in the "Wicked Bible" of 1641?
    A. Thou shalt kill
    B. Thou shalt steal
    C. Thou shalt commit adultery
    D. Thou shalt covet

97. Francis Xavier became a missionary because of losing a bet to Ignatius Loyola. The bet was that if Francis lost, he had to examine his life. What game did they bet on?
    A. Billiards
    B. Blackjack
    C. Chess
    D. Fencing

98. Which of the following is not part of the William Penn list that begins, "No pain, no palm"?
    A. No thorns, no throne
    B. No gall, no glory
    C. No help, no hope
    D. No cross, no crown

99. What aspect of contemporary church seating would be most likely to astonish a fourth-century Christian?
    A. People sit during the sermon
    B. Men and women are allowed to sit in the same section
    C. Children and adults are allowed to sit in the same section
    D. The seats face the Communion table

100. Why did Nero have some early Christians soaked in oil?
    A. It was a form of anointing, a great honor
    B. He was running an experiment on evaporation rates
    C. He used them as torches for his garden parties
    D. Peasants had to be cleansed before entering the emperor's presence, and oil was their cleaning agent

101. What British poet first commented that God did
not make woman out of man's head to be over
him or out of man's foot to be under him but out
of man's rib to be beside him?
   A. Geoffrey Chaucer
   B. William Shakespeare
   C. William Wordsworth
   D. Robert Browning

102. What is the earliest mention of a church choir?
   A. 107
   B. 307
   C. 507
   D. 707

103. What did the word "tething," from which we get
"tithing," mean?
   A. A tenth of one's money
   B. A tenth of one's crops
   C. A special pasture where the fattest
       sheep were tethered
   D. A district containing ten families

104. What is a jihad?
   A. The Moslem term for a holy war
   B. The Hindi term for the spirit that is
       reincarnated from body to body
   C. The Buddhist term for spiritual
       enlightenment
   D. The Shinto term for emperor worship

105. Squanto had a lot to forgive the Europeans for.
They did all of the following to him except which?

A. Although Squanto wanted to return to
his family, the English held him cap-
tive for nine years

B. The English sold him to the Spanish as
a slave

C. European diseases killed off every
person in his entire village

D. When Squanto tried to return to the
Pilgrims after six months, they shot at
and wounded him

106. The colony governor called Squanto "a special
instrument sent by God" because he did all of the
following except which?

A. He caught eels with his bare hands to
feed the colony

B. He stole seed corn from the Indians
and gave it to the colonists

C. He prevented Indian attacks by saying
the Pilgrims kept barrels of diseases
inside their fort

D. He showed the colonists how to con-
struct log cabins

107. Most people have heard of Squanto, but few know much about him. For example, what was Squanto's religious persuasion?
    A. Calvinist
    B. Arminian
    C. Unitarian
    D. Pantheistic until his deathbed conversion to Christianity

108. According to Pope Innocent III, what is the relationship of a king to the pope like?
    A. A drop of water to the ocean
    B. The moon to the sun
    C. A shadow to the sun
    D. Regular wine to Communion wine

109. For a thousand years Scripture was interpreted by the "four-layer" method. Water, besides its literal meaning, was taken to stand for all of the following except which?
    A. Baptism (allegorical)
    B. Wisdom (moral)
    C. Eternal happiness (spiritual)
    D. The Flood (hyperbolical)

110. What nationwide radio talk show hosted by
     Marlin Maddoux was accused of being "more
     Republican than Christian"?
     A. "Focus on the Family"
     B. "In Touch"
     C. "Point of View"
     D. "The Hour of Power"

SECTION 7

1. Benedictine monks used sign language so they could eat their meals in silence (while someone read aloud to the group). All the following are signs; which is mustard?
   A. A thumb enclosed in a fist
   B. Pulling on the left little finger
   C. Flicking with the right thumb over the left thumb
   D. Holding one's nose in the right fist

2. Which of the following magazines is not associated with Christianity Today, Inc.?
   A. *Leadership*
   B. *Partnership*
   C. *Moody Monthly*
   D. *Campus Life*

3. Among churches using Sunday School pins, for what year of perfect attendance does one receive a wreath?
   A. First
   B. Second
   C. Third
   D. Fourth

4. Which of the following songs has a question in the chorus?
   A. " 'Are Ye Able?' Said the Master"
   B. "Have You Any Room for Jesus"?
   C. "What Can Wash Away My Sin"?
   D. "Are You Washed in the Blood"?

5. What is the Authorised Version of the Bible called in the United States?
   A. Revised Standard
   B. American Standard
   C. King James
   D. New International

6. Where did the terms "High Mass" and "Low Mass" come from?
   A. How high the priest held the Eucharist
   B. How loud part of the service was
   C. What status the worshipers were
   D. What portion of time the worshipers had to stand

7. In what C. S. Lewis book is there a character named C. S. Lewis?
   A. *Perelandra*
   B. *Till We Have Faces*
   C. *Prince Caspian*
   D. *The Silver Chair*

8. What Shakespearian play is considered his most
   "Christian" for its resurrection and redemption
   images?
   A. *As You Like It*
   B. *All's Well That Ends Well*
   C. *Measure for Measure*
   D. *The Tempest*

9. Why are there no New Testament books as long
   as the longest Old Testament books?
   A. There was an ink shortage in the
      Roman Empire
   B. There was a papyrus shortage in the
      Roman Empire
   C. The papyrus rolls used in the first
      century could not hold too many
      words
   D. According to Jewish tradition, it was
      inappropriate to write any work longer
      than Genesis

10. What Amy Grant song deals with spiritual imma-
    turity?
    A. "Angels"
    B. "Fat Baby"
    C. "In a Little While"
    D. "All I Ever Have To Be"

11. How did Katherine von Bora, Martin Luther's future wife, escape from her convent?
    A. She was carried out in a herring barrel
    B. She shaved her head and dressed as a friar
    C. She jumped from the wall and landed on mattresses that friends had placed there for her
    D. She didn't escape. She simply said it was God's will for her to go, and they let her

12. Ansgar, medieval missionary to the Danes, was often praised for his alleged miracles. What was Ansgar's standard response?
    A. Thank you
    B. Even Satan can work miracles
    C. The greatest miracle will be if God ever makes me a good man
    D. You will see greater wonders than these if your clans ever begin to love one another

13. The year 1859 is sometimes called the golden year of literature because four authors each published perhaps their greatest work that year. Which one affected Christianity most?
    A. Tennyson's *Idylls of the King*
    B. Browning's *The Ring and the Book*
    C. Eliot's *Adam Bede*
    D. Darwin's *Origin of Species*

14. What unusual decision stimulated John Fawcett to write "Blest Be the Tie That Binds"?
    A. He turned down the pastorate of a larger church with a bigger salary
    B. He was hired to be a white church's pastor even though he was black
    C. He and his wife decided to remarry after their divorce
    D. He was able to get his teenage son to wear a tie to church

15. With what Christian movement are Raymond and Dorothy Moore most closely associated?
    A. Pro-life efforts
    B. Sunday schools
    C. Simple lifestyle
    D. Home schooling

16. What did Muhammed-ad-Dhib find in a cave in 1947?
    A. Stalactites and stalagmites
    B. The hidden plans for the creation of Israel as a country in 1948
    C. The Codex Sinaiticus
    D. The Dead Sea Scrolls

17. How many relics (alleged souvenirs of famous religious people) did Wittenberg have when Luther began preaching against them? (Note: If it will help your calculations, the 204 body parts of babies killed by Herod were counted as separate items.)
   A. 1,100
   B. 3,800
   C. 11,000
   D. 19,000

18. A person paying to view all these relics in Wittenberg would escape how many years of purgatory?
   A. 200
   B. 2,000
   C. 200,000
   D. 2,000,000

19. What was Roger Williams's (founder of Rhode Island) principle of "soul-liberty"?
   A. A person can do whatever he wants and still be saved
   B. The community cannot punish private sins
   C. A person may be put in prison, but his spirit is still free
   D. A community needs more than one church so people have a choice of where to worship

20. What is the literal meaning of the Latin "a cappella"?
    A. Without a cloak
    B. Without a building
    C. Without instruments
    D. Without a cap

21. When Christ called the church at Laodicea luke-warm, He was apparently referring to a civic problem. What archaeological evidence is there that the drinking water at Laodicea was not cold?
    A. Other large Roman cities have hot and cold faucets; Laodicean households have only lukewarm faucets
    B. Expense accounts of wealthy Laodicean households show large amounts spent for ice
    C. At least four extant Latin plays contain the proverb "warm as water in Laodicea"
    D. The water pipes in Laodicea are encrusted with calcium carbonate

22. Which of these would be an appropriate subject for a medieval mystery play?
    A. The life of Noah
    B. The life of Gregory the Great
    C. The life of "Everyman"
    D. The thoughts of God

23. In the early twentieth century, many church pianists learned to recognize notes by distinctive shapes. In treble clef in a shaped-noted hymnal, what shape is "D"?
    A. A diamond
    B. A right triangle
    C. An equilateral triangle
    D. A rectangle

24. What was the original meaning of "ghetto"?
    A. The place where Christians were required to live
    B. The place where Jews were required to live
    C. The place where Moslems were required to live
    D. The area around a black church; it had to be built at least a mile from the nearest white church

25. The oldest partial New Testament manuscript is a portion of the Gospel of John. What is this manuscript's approximate date?
    A. 130
    B. 230
    C. 330
    D. 430

26. "A man small in size, with meeting eyebrows and a rather large nose, bald-headed, bow-legged, strongly built." Who is this a description of?
    A. Paul
    B. Martin Luther
    C. C. S. Lewis
    D. Chuck Swindoll

27. "One short sleep past, we wake eternally/ And death shall be no more; death, thou shalt die." Who is the author of this sonnet?
    A. Edmund Spenser
    B. William Shakespeare
    C. John Donne
    D. Alfred Tennyson

28. How many times does one hear the phrase "fly away" if listening to a congregation singing the first verse and chorus of "I'll Fly Away"?
    A. Seven
    B. Nine
    C. Eleven
    D. Thirteen

29. The early Christians often referred to Communion as Eucharist. What does Eucharist mean?
    A. Short for "You are Christ"
    B. True wine
    C. Thanksgiving
    D. Fellowship

30. Famed New England preacher Jonathan Edwards died of smallpox in March of 1758. What was unusual about that?
    A. He publicly prayed for God to protect Southhampton from the smallpox plague, and no one died except him
    B. He was inoculated against smallpox in February of 1758
    C. In 1752, he publicly said God had revealed to him that he would die in 1758
    D. His middle name was Patrick, just like his father and grandfather, and they all died on St. Patrick's Day

31. In the twentieth century, has the percentage of Americans who are church members generally gone up, down, or stayed the same?
    A. Up
    B. Down
    C. Stayed the same
    D. None of the above. It went steadily up the first half of the century and has gone down the second half

32. "Fadir, the our cometh. Clarifie thy sone, that this one clarifie thee." This is the opening of John 17; what translation is it?
    A. Wycliffe
    B. Geneva
    C. Bishops'
    D. King James

33. What was unusual about how medieval theology students paid their professors?
    A. They didn't; the professors paid the students for the privilege of having listeners
    B. They bought each course by the class, paying for it at the end of each class session
    C. They had the option of paying in money or paying in prayers (to shorten the professor's time in Purgatory)
    D. They only had to pay if they received a church post after graduation (ten percent of annual salary for five years)

34. What was Alexander Cruden noted for?
    A. On June 8, 1922, in Oklahoma City, Oklahoma, he became the nation's first radio preacher
    B. In 1884, he became the first preacher to issue an invitation at the end of every church service
    C. He founded Cruden Christian College
    D. He put together a concordance to help people find Bible verses

35. In some fourth-century churches cheering
    occurred during the worship service. Whom were
    the people cheering?
    A. People who got baptized
    B. God
    C. Preachers who preached good sermons
    D. Preachers who preached short sermons

36. "For God did not give us a spirit of timidity—of
    cowardice, of craven and cringing and fawning
    fear." What translation is this of 2 Timothy 1:7a?
    A. King James
    B. New American Standard
    C. New International
    D. Amplified

37. What was John Wesley's explanation of why
    spiritual revivals can't last?
    A. Converts work harder and spend less,
       which makes them rich, which makes
       them lose interest in Christianity
    B. People who get excited about
       Christianity start out praying but
       wind up working, which seems more
       effective
    C. People who are not radically Christian
       seem so much more reasonable that
       they tend to cool off converts
    D. The revival generation meets Christ
       personally, while the next generally
       only hears stories about Him

38. Which of the following was not one of the three
    most popular destinations for pilgrimages in
    medieval Europe?
    A. Santiago de Compostela, Spain
    B. Rome, Italy
    C. Canterbury, England
    D. Paris, France

39. What Communist leader was at one time a semi-
    nary student?
    A. Lenin
    B. Trotsky
    C. Stalin
    D. Kruschev

40. Virtually everyone knows Notre Dame
    University. But what does Notre Dame mean?
    A. North Land
    B. Our Lady
    C. Give To Us
    D. Noted Woman

41. "I look upon everyone who dies in it as a mar-
    tyr." The bishop of London said this about which
    war?
    A. The Third Crusade
    B. The Revolutionary War
    C. World War I
    D. World War II

42. List the churches below in order of how often they generally offer Communion to their members, beginning with the church that tends to offer Communion most frequently.
    A. Church of Christ, Anglican, Quaker, Presbyterian
    B. Church of Christ, Presbyterian, Quaker, Anglican
    C. Church of Christ, Presbyterian, Anglican, Quaker
    D. Anglican, Church of Christ, Presbyterian, Quaker

43. The first New Testament canon (list of books) was put together about 140 by Marcion. What was unusual about him?
    A. He was blind
    B. He had only been a Christian about six months
    C. He was a Gnostic rather than a Christian
    D. To the best of our knowledge, he was the last person to have known one of the apostles personally (John)

44. What group became famous for unusually named converts such as Sarah McMinnies the Saved Barmaid and Happy Hannah the Reformed Smoker?
    A. The American Temperance Movement
    B. The Salvation Army
    C. The early Methodists
    D. The Quakers

45. In the fourth century the church began pressuring
    clergy to be single. This caused two great abuses,
    one being single clergymen living with women.
    What was the other?
    A. Secret marriages, which meant that
       after the clergyman's death the wife
       inherited nothing
    B. Clergymen castrated themselves to
       remove sexual temptation
    C. Husbands deserted their wives to
       become priests
    D. Married priests were asked to recant
       their wives. Those who refused had
       their wives killed by the church

46. How, according to Isaac Newton, do the planets
    stay in their orbits?
    A. At their creation God set them spin-
       ning perfectly forever
    B. God directly intervenes and makes
       minor adjustments when He discovers
       the planets getting out of line
    C. God assigns an angel to guard the orbit
       of each planet; it gives the angels
       something to do
    D. The planets are kept in their orbits
       simply by the combination of centrifu-
       gal force and gravitational pull

47. We all know that Ferdinand and Isabella sent out Columbus in 1492, but they also took a significant religious action in that same year. What was it?
    A. They halted the Spanish Inquisition
    B. They expelled all Jews from Spain
    C. They began the building of the Compostela Cathedral
    D. They sponsored the first translation of the Bible into Spanish

48. What was Frenchman Gustave Dore's major contribution to twentieth-century family Bibles?
    A. He is a frequently used illustrator
    B. He came up with the idea of having a family tree in the Bible
    C. He developed the padded cover
    D. He began the "pyramid system" of Bible sales in Europe

49. What did Russian cosmonaut Yuri Gagarin remark when he returned from space?
    A. "I did not see God out there"
    B. "I now believe that Someone or Something must have made all this"
    C. "I have much to think about"
    D. "I am now convinced of the superiority of man to any other being in the universe"

50. What physical handicap did hymnwriter Fanny
    Crosby have?
    A. Paraplegia
    B. Quadriplegia
    C. Deafness
    D. Blindness

51. Where was Archbishop of Canterbury Thomas a
    Becket murdered?
    A. In his study while preparing a sermon
       on love
    B. In the home of a peasant to whom he
       had just given alms
    C. In a house of prostitution
    D. At the altar of his cathedral

52. If one is speaking of a French cathedral (as
    opposed to an American football team), how does
    one pronounce "Dame" in "Notre Dame"?
    A. It rhymes with "came"
    B. It rhymes with "jam"
    C. It rhymes with "mom"
    D. It rhymes with "Camay" (the soap)

53. What was one of the chief obstacles in the way of the Vikings being converted to Christianity?
    A. The Vikings loved horsemeat, and missionaries said true Christians wouldn't eat horsemeat
    B. The Vikings liked to put dragons on the front of their ships, and missionaries said that was satanic
    C. The Vikings liked to wear hats with horns, and missionaries said those were satanic
    D. The Vikings let their toenails grow, and missionaries said true Christians trimmed their toenails

54. A Bible is sitting on the coffee table of an American home. Does it have a book in it called Ecclesiasticus?
    A. Yes
    B. No
    C. Maybe, but probably not
    D. Probably, but not necessarily

55. "Congress shall make no law respecting an establishment of religion or prohibiting the free exercise thereof." Which amendment is this?
    A. First
    B. Second
    C. Third
    D. Fourth

56. In Laurence Sterne's famous phrase, God tempers
    the wind to what?
    A. The shorn lamb
    B. The bleating calf
    C. The bald man
    D. The house of straw

57. The first famous religious hermit, an Egyptian
    monk named Antony, virtually lived on bread and
    water. What was the only other thing he ate?
    A. Grass
    B. Locusts
    C. Figs
    D. Salt

58. What are icons?
    A. Religious paintings or sculptures
    B. Small pebbles used by monks to keep
       a tally of their daily sins
    C. Eskimo churches constructed out of ice
    D. Bible incidents once thought fictional
       that have been proven true by
       archaeology

59. *Dios Habla Hoy* is the Good News translation of
    the Bible into what language?
    A. German
    B. Spanish
    C. French
    D. Esperanto

60. Mr. Valiant-for-Truth said: "I am going to my father's, and though with great difficulty I am got hither, yet now I do not repent." What is this from?
    A. *The Imitation of Christ*
    B. *Paradise Regained*
    C. *Pilgrim's Progress*
    D. *Idylls of the King*

61. What was the artistic style of Counter-Reformation artists, such as sculptor Lorenzo Bernini and writer Richard Crashaw, a style noted for its lavish excesses?
    A. Imagism
    B. Realism
    C. Baroque
    D. Pathetique

62. "Just as I am! without one plea." But actually, according to this hymn's lyrics, the sinner has two pleas. One is Jesus' blood; what is the other?
    A. The words of Scripture
    B. His own changed heart
    C. Jesus' resurrection
    D. Jesus' request to come

63. Which of these is a book in the Apocrypha?
    A. Tabitha
    B. Dorothea
    C. Elizabeth
    D. Judith

64. "Just-war" advocates maintain that several questions must be answered affirmatively before a Christian nation can enter a war. Which of these is not a just-war question?
    A. Is the war being declared by a legitimate authority?
    B. Will war be likely to cause less damage than peace would?
    C. Does the nation we are fighting claim to be Christian?
    D. Are we likely to win?

65. "Swords of iron we leave to those who, alas, consider human blood and swine's blood to be of well-nigh equal value." The man who said this founded what group?
    A. Baptists
    B. Mennonites
    C. Assemblies of God
    D. Disciples of Christ

66. Complete this William Inge quote: "If we spend sixteen hours a day dealing with tangible things and only five minutes a day dealing with God. . .
    A. . . . we're right at the national average"
    B. . . . we need to set aside one day a week to reverse those figures"
    C. . . . it's time to call a misdeal"
    D. . . . is it any wonder tangible things are 200 times more real to us than God"?

67. The early Quakers believed people should be entirely led by the Spirit. What did Quaker James Naylor feel led to do in Bristol, England, that created a national scandal?
    A. He had a woman pretend to give birth to him in a stable
    B. He had a triumphal entry complete with donkey and hosannas
    C. He had himself crucified
    D. He had friends seal him in a tomb for three days and almost died from lack of oxygen

68. What Naylor did (previous question) was considered blasphemous, and blasphemers were punished severely in the 1700s. Naylor received all the following punishments except which?
    A. He was whipped and imprisoned
    B. He was branded with a B on his forehead (for blasphemer)
    C. He had a hole bored in his tongue with a hot iron
    D. He had his foot crushed in the "iron boot," which caused him to walk with a limp for the rest of his life

69. What was the largest American denomination at the start of the Civil War?
    A. Methodist
    B. Baptist
    C. Presbyterian
    D. Catholic

70. One of the earliest writers to try to explain Christ's relationship to God the Father was Tertullian. How did he do it?
    A. Christ is to God as a ray is to the sun
    B. Christ is to God as a drop of water is to the ocean
    C. Christ is to God as a kernel of corn is to the stalk
    D. Christ is to God as spring is to winter

71. In what century was the first Bible commentary printed?
    A. Twelfth
    B. Fourteenth
    C. Sixteenth
    D. Eighteenth

72. People in the eighth century who fought icons (religious images) argued that only five things on earth are holy, preachers being one. Which did they call holiest of all?
    A. Communion elements
    B. Bibles
    C. Crosses
    D. Churches

73. Which of the following was not a church office in the Roman church of A.D. 250?
    A. Exorcist
    B. Reader
    C. Doorkeeper
    D. Candlelighter

74. When is the first definite mention of a child's being baptized (as opposed to an infant or adult)?
    A. Early second century
    B. Early third century
    C. Early fourth century
    D. Early fifth century

75. "God doth not need/ Either man's work or His own gifts. Who best/ Bear His mild yoke, they serve Him best. . . They also serve who only stand and wait." Who wrote this?
    A. John Milton
    B. John Bunyan
    C. Robert Browning
    D. Robert Frost

76. Augustine once sent two disputing clergymen to the shrine of Felix of Nola. What was Felix the patron saint of?
    A. Arguing
    B. Peacemaking
    C. Wisdom
    D. Lie detection

77. Which of these was not one of the three main criteria the church considered for including books in the New Testament?
    A. Was it written or approved by an apostle?
    B. Is its content orthodox?
    C. Does it include a quotation from the Old Testament?
    D. Is it publicly used by prominent churches?

78. Eighteenth-century evangelist George Whitefield was famous for the fervency of his sermons. What complaint was made to the bishop after Whitefield's first sermon?
    A. He had allegedly driven fifteen people insane
    B. The congregation, mostly laborers, was not able to get in their Sunday morning sleep
    C. Whitefield's voice flaked down plaster from the ceiling onto the congregation
    D. Fifty-eight people came forward to be saved, but they were all already members of the congregation

79. Adolph Hitler was raised as a member of the Catholic church. At what point did the church excommunicate him?
    A. When he declared war on Poland
    B. When he removed the church's tax exemption
    C. When he sent the Archbishop of Dusseldorf to the gas chamber
    D. Never

80. "A God without wrath brought men without sin into a kingdom without judgment." What is Richard Niebuhr describing?
    A. The Book of Romans
    B. Evangelical theology
    C. Liberal theology
    D. Modern psychology's views of religion

81. Approximately what percentage of his book income did C. S. Lewis generally give away to charity?
    A. Ten
    B. Thirty
    C. Fifty
    D. Seventy

82. The Ethiopian eunuch was converted by a man in
    the desert whom he never saw before or (as far as
    we know) again. What early church father was
    converted the same way?
    A. Justin Martyr
    B. Tertullian
    C. Polycarp
    D. Augustine

83. All of these are parts of early church buildings
    except which?
    A. Apse
    B. Aisle
    C. Nave
    D. Furze

84. Which of the following hymns is most fitting for
    a funeral?
    A. "Jesus Is Calling"
    B. "I Am Coming, Lord"
    C. "Lead Me to Calvary"
    D. "Some Day the Silver Cord Will
       Break"

85. Which of these Christian books was turned into
    an acclaimed 1988 CBS-TV movie?
    A. *A Taste of New Wine*
    B. *At Least We Were Married*
    C. *We Let Our Son Die*
    D. *Come before Winter*

86. Pope Stephen VI didn't like the man who had preceded him as pope, so he put his predecessor on trial. What was the most unusual feature of the trial?
    A. They dug up the (dead) previous pope's body and propped it up in a chair so it could defend itself
    B. They found the (living) previous pope's body innocent of sin but his head guilty of heresy, so they chopped off his head
    C. The (dead) previous pope's bones refused to burn, so they became the most valuable relics of the medieval church
    D. Stephen had a heart attack during the trial, so the (living) previous pope returned to office

87. What famous preacher was a wartime double agent?
    A. Charles Spurgeon
    B. David Lipscomb
    C. Billy Sunday
    D. Dietrich Bonhoeffer

88. Which of these would be a typical name for a character in a medieval morality play?
    A. Barnabas
    B. St. Benedict
    C. Mr. Love-the-World
    D. Ralph Roister-Doister

89. The oldest known depiction of the Crucifixion, done about 430, is unusual because the cross is missing, making Christ appear to hang in midair. What else is unusual about it?
    A. Christ is hanging upside-down
    B. It is the first picture to give Christ a beard
    C. It is the first picture of Christ with a halo
    D. There are no wounds in Christ's hands, feet, or side

90. In medieval theology, what location was developed for virtuous pagans and unbaptized infants?
    A. Akimbo
    B. Limbo
    C. Mumbo
    D. Rambo

91. Thomas Aquinas's family did not want him to become a Dominican friar. To stop him, they did all the following except which?
    A. Kidnapped him
    B. Offered him a prostitute
    C. Prayed to God to make him "normal"
    D. Offered to buy him a high-paying job as an archbishop

92. What writer first referred to prayer as "conversation with God"?
    A. Philip Yancey
    B. Robert Schuller
    C. Rosalind Rinker
    D. Clement of Alexandria

93. Halloween is the day before a religious holiday. Which holiday?
    A. Pentecost
    B. Passover
    C. All Saints' Day
    D. Ash Wednesday

94. Approximately how tall is France's Notre Dame Cathedral?
    A. 55 feet
    B. 85 feet
    C. 115 feet
    D. 145 feet

95. The eighteenth century's most famous actor, David Garrick, said about George Whitefield's voice, "I would give a hundred guineas if I could say ___ like Mr. Whitefield." What word is missing?
    A. Wombat
    B. Articulate
    C. Oh
    D. Israel

96. Quaker leader John Woolman was the first major American religious figure to fight against slavery. What was his nonviolent method of protest?
    A. He was able to raise enough money to buy and free every slave auctioned in Georgia for five years
    B. Whenever he was at someone's home where a slave waited on him, he always paid the slave
    C. He spread rumors that the slave ships were carrying diseases, which cut down importation of slaves
    D. He got all American Quakers to refuse to wear cotton

97. What is the biggest worldwide sociological shift in Christianity over the past two centuries?
    A. There used to be far more male Christians than female; now that is reversed
    B. The overwhelming majority of Christians used to be Caucasian; that is no longer the case
    C. The average age at baptism has gone down steadily; it is now less than half of what it used to be
    D. Christianity used to be the world's largest religion; it has dropped one place each century

98. Over the years a large number of individuals have been identified with the antichrist. Who was most commonly given that label in the seventh and eighth centuries?
    A. The pope
    B. Charlemagne
    C. Kublai Khan
    D. Mohammed

99. What is a parallel Bible?
    A. A Bible that has the outer edge parallel to its spine
    B. A Bible put out with different wording for different denominations
    C. A Bible that shows similarities between the Old and New Testaments
    D. A Bible that includes more than one translation

100. Amy Grant's album *Unguarded* generated more criticism than any other contemporary Christian album. Which of the following was she not criticized about?
    A. Her pose on the cover of the album
    B. The lyrics not being "religious" enough
    C. Her use of rouge and eye shadow
    D. The album's airplay on secular stations

CHURCH CHALLENGE

101. In A.D. 250 the church in Rome had one bishop. How many elders and deacons did it have?
    A. One elder and sixty-six deacons
    B. Forty-six elders and seven deacons
    C. Seven elders and forty-six deacons
    D. One hundred twenty deacons—the office of elder had been eliminated

102. David Livingstone was the first man to travel clear across the continent of Africa by what method?
    A. On foot
    B. On horseback
    C. On a bicycle
    D. By canoe

103. The Roman Empire's first edict regarding observance of Sunday mentioned four groups. Three were expected to rest on Sundays; which group was exempted from the law?
    A. Judges
    B. Craftsmen
    C. City dwellers
    D. Farmers

104. According to Mark Twain, the harp and the psalm are as inseparable as what?
    A. A comb and a brush
    B. A comb and a mirror
    C. Hair and a brush
    D. A pair of pants

105. What is the importance of fourth-century writer Eusebius to this book?
    A. He was the first to use together the words "Church Challenge" (in Greek)
    B. He wrote the first comprehensive history of the church
    C. In a letter to Gregory of Nazianzus, Eusebius came up with the idea of a Bible trivia contest
    D. He first came up with the idea of Christian bookstores

106. Many Christians believed God was putting an end to the world in the 1360s. Why?
    A. The bubonic plague
    B. The Viking raids
    C. The seventh (and last) year of the Great European Famine
    D. The failure of the Eighth Crusade to stop Moslem advances

107. In early Benedictine monasteries the sick were allowed certain privileges. Which of the following was not a privilege of the sick?
    A. Eating meat
    B. Taking extra baths
    C. Being excused from kitchen work
    D. Leaving the monastery to visit a doctor

108. What eighteenth-century group spent so much time studying the Scriptures that they gained the nickname "Bible Moths"?
    A. Baptists
    B. Lutherans
    C. Methodists
    D. Presbyterians

109. Southern gospel singer Christy Lane became most famous for a song in which she asks Christ, "Help me to pray/ Teach me to take/. . ." What?
    A. "You into my heart"
    B. "All You have for me"
    C. "One day at a time"
    D. "The goodness of life"

110. What is the significance of "Didache" (pronounced did-uh-kay)?
    A. It was the last book ever to be written in Koine (New Testament) Greek
    B. He was the soldier on whom the movie *Ben Hur* was based
    C. That was the Greek code word for the Roman assault on Jerusalem in A.D. 70
    D. It was a second-century book of Christian teaching, not discovered until 1873

ANSWERS

SECTION 1 (page 5)

1. C
2. A (He neglected to copyright it; some publishers voluntarily gave him money anyway.)
3. A
4. B
5. D (better known as Amy Grant)
6. D
7. D
8. A
9. A
10. C
11. A
12. B
13. A
14. C
15. A
16. D
17. B
18. C
19. D
20. A (He was wrong.)
21. C
22. B
23. B
24. A
25. D
26. D
27. C
28. B
29. D
30. D
31. A
32. D (Nazarene)
33. A
34. C
35. A
36. B
37. C
38. D
39. A
40. C
41. D
42. A
43. B
44. C
45. C
46. B
47. C
48. A (Cologne Cathedral, 512 feet)
49. D
50. D (Standard practice in the eastern Roman Empire was to leave the church one-third of the inheritance.)

51. A (Luther's friend Jonas Justus said, "As I watched this spectacle I could not hold back my tears.")
52. D
53. B
54. C
55. B
56. D
57. A
58. B
59. D (all but Maryland)
60. C
61. A
62. A
63. D
64. B
65. C
66. A (Some sources call it a mosquito bite; in either case, it ulcerated and pained him the rest of his life.)
67. C
68. B
69. D
70. A
71. B
72. A
73. D
74. B
75. C
76. B
77. D
78. C
79. C
80. C (The phrase "under God" is not used.)
81. A
82. B
83. C
84. A
85. B
86. D
87. A
88. B
89. A
90. C
91. A (from J. R. R. Tolkien's *The Hobbit*)
92. C
93. A
94. B
95. D (That was how Lewis got the name for his Christ-figure in the *Chronicles of Narnia*.)
96. B
97. A

98. B
99. B
100. B
101. A
102. D
103. C
104. A
105. D
106. D
107. B
108. B (Sometimes they used cheeses or other foods as well.)
109. C
110. D

SECTION 2 (page 40)

1. C
2. D
3. B
4. D
5. A
6. B
7. C
8. B
9. C (because people who could read were sometimes too valuable to be killed for a first offense)
10. B (The Christians refused.)
11. C
12. A
13. D
14. A
15. D
16. D
17. A
18. D
19. D
20. A
21. A
22. D
23. C
24. B
25. C
26. C
27. C (I "scarce" can take it in rather than "scarcely.")
28. A (or the third, whichever happens to be Super Bowl Sunday)
29. B
30. A
31. B
32. A
33. D
34. A
35. D (Ronald Reagan over Jimmy Carter)

36. B
37. A
38. D
39. A
40. D
41. C
42. A
43. B
44. B
45. C
46. D
47. A
48. D ("A" might be true as well!)
49. D (Harriet Beecher Stowe)
50. D
51. D (They generally had a priestly representative at lower pay.)
52. B
53. C
54. B
55. A
56. A
57. A
58. C
59. A
60. C
61. C
62. D

63. C
64. A
65. D
66. C
67. D
68. C
69. B
70. A
71. A
72. A (His proposal was soundly defeated.)
73. B
74. C (Previously jailers extorted their pay from the prisoners they kept.)
75. D
76. C
77. D
78. B
79. C
80. C
81. A
82. D
83. A
84. B ("D" might be true as well.)
85. B
86. D
87. C
88. B
89. C

90. B (Some have noted a resemblance to contemporary pot luck dinners here.)
91. A
92. D
93. C
94. A (for "cleric")
95. C
96. B
97. B
98. A
99. A
100. A
101. B (to fit into the Chinese culture)
102. B
103. A
104. D (from Julius Caesar)
105. A
106. C
107. D
108. D
109. C
110. B

SECTION 3 (page 77)

1. D
2. D
3. D
4. C
5. C
6. D
7. A
8. B
9. B
10. A
11. A
12. A
13. C
14. D
15. A
16. B
17. A
18. B
19. A
20. C
21. D (Around 600 despair was replaced by envy, but now despair is reappearing on some contemporary lists.)
22. B
23. D (Drowning was a common form of execution for Anabaptists, as a way of punishing them for believing in immersion.)

24. C
25. B
26. D
27. C (by C. S. Lewis)
28. A (It's called the "Lactation of the Virgin.")
29. B
30. D
31. A
32. A
33. A
34. A
35. C (The bishop collected 7,500 guilders one year, which would indicate his priests fathered 1875 children!)
36. B
37. D
38. A
39. D (Girls were not allowed to attend public schools.)
40. C
41. B
42. B
43. A (In the fourth century, silent reading was virtually unknown.)

44. D
45. D (To better appreciate this feat, note that if a man preached fifteen sermons a week every week for fifty years, he would still come up short of Wesley's figure.)
46. C (So many people died that thousands lost their faith in God's goodness.)
47. D
48. B (Increase and Cotton)
49. D
50. A
51. B
52. B (Latin "ad venire")
53. A (96 hours. Others have only seemed that long.)
54. C
55. D
56. A (Charles said someone needed to be uncovered in the king's presence.)
57. C
58. D

59. B
60. D ("D" was true of his first marriage, however.)
61. C
62. C (Teaching evolution was illegal whether one taught creation with it or not.)
63. C
64. A
65. A
66. C
67. A
68. B (Wesley's parents argued about whether William was a usurper, so Samuel pledged never to have marital relations with Susanna till they agreed. Eventually William died. About nine months later, John was born.)
69. A
70. D
71. C
72. B
73. D
74. B
75. B
76. A
77. D
78. C
79. B
80. A (Thousands of Christians expected Him because a "millennium" had passed since His birth.)
81. A
82. D
83. C
84. D (Madelyn's son)
85. B
86. A
87. B
88. C
89. B
90. D
91. A
92. D
93. C
94. A
95. B (the Lion-Hearted)
96. B (because he had said that if people didn't send in enough money, the Lord would "call him home")

97. D
98. B
99. D
100. C
101. D
102. C
103. A
104. D
105. C
106. B
107. D (The two opening lines were the same; then these followed.)
108. A
109. B
110. D

SECTION 4 (page 112)

1. C
2. A
3. A
4. C (Midrash refers to "fleshing out" a story with additional dialogue.)
5. B (Times have changed.)
6. D
7. A
8. C
9. A
10. B
11. D
12. B
13. C
14. A
15. D
16. A
17. C
18. D (It is located in Augsburg, Germany.)
19. B
20. C
21. B
22. B
23. C
24. C
25. C (sometimes phrased "till they rest in Thee")
26. D
27. B
28. C
29. D
30. A
31. A
32. A
33. A (because he was so big and took so long to answer questions)

34. B (Lazy pastors were presenting skimpy sermons, and people wanted to make sure they got their money's worth.)
35. C
36. D
37. A
38. C (Salvation Army, that is)
39. C
40. D (19 were Susanna's; many of the 44 died in infancy)
41. A and B
42. B
43. C
44. D
45. D
46. D (Commentators note that Milton in this poem seems to have confused Jesus with himself.)
47. D
48. C
49. A (by Thomas Aquinas)
50. C (Thus people could see how the Book of Mormon has changed.)
51. B (When one teenage girl objected to playing a "granny," the annoyed Ida beat her in straight sets.)
52. D
53. C
54. A (the Hebrew Old Testament into Greek)
55. D
56. B
57. B
58. C
59. A
60. D
61. A
62. D
63. C
64. B
65. C
66. D
67. B ("B" is by humorist Erma Bombeck.)
68. D
69. A
70. A
71. B
72. C
73. D (dunce)

74. A (because it said Adam and Eve went out and made themselves "breeches")
75. B
76. D
77. C
78. D
79. C
80. D
81. D (Acts 19:27)
82. C
83. C
84. C
85. D
86. D (6,500 of them were set to music.)
87. C (There had been national days of thanksgiving before, but they weren't legal holidays.)
88. C
89. A
90. A (The boycott, led by people upset that poor mothers in impoverished countries were buying formula instead of breast feeding, ended in 1982.)
91. B ("His Eye Is on the Sparrow")
92. D (from about 400–1600)
93. A (Another saint had lost part of her breast and a fingertip to relic collectors while still alive.)
94. C
95. B (He allegedly said he wasn't worthy to be crucified like Jesus.)
96. D
97. B (from 12,000 to nearly 5,000,000)
98. B
99. D
100. D
101. A
102. C
103. B (Codex Sinaiticus)
104. C
105. D
106. C
107. A (An owl stands for Satan.)
108. B
109. A
110. D

Section 5 (page 147)

1. B (At that time most people had to pay for their church pews; it made money and kept the church upper and middle-class.)
2. C
3. C
4. D
5. D
6. C
7. B
8. A
9. A
10. B ("Whiter Than Snow," "Master the Tempest Is Raging," and "There Shall Be Showers of Blessings")
11. A
12. D (The first three words mean "crib.")
13. C
14. A
15. A
16. A
17. B (because of a belief that they were "graven images")
18. C
19. A
20. C
21. B
22. D
23. D
24. B
25. A (The repeated word is "joy.")
26. B
27. C
28. C
29. D
30. C
31. D (Regarding "C," she was given another bath before her burial.)
32. B (from about 320–400)
33. B
34. D
35. C
36. D
37. A (*Morning and Evening* is a devotional by Charles Spurgeon)
38. A (because they are being purified for heaven)
39. D

40. D
41. A
42. B
43. D
44. C
45. C
46. B
47. B (The landlord got the best beast. The church of that day robbed widows and orphans rather than protecting them.)
48. C
49. D
50. A
51. A
52. A
53. D
54. C
55. B
56. D
57. C
58. C
59. A
60. D
61. D
62. B
63. B
64. A
65. C
66. C (*Love Must be Tough* is by Christian pyschologist James Dobson.)
67. A
68. C (Many people say "trespasses.")
69. B
70. C
71. C
72. D (His father bought the positions for John as moneymakers, and they hired unemployed priests at low salaries for the actual work.)
73. B
74. A
75. C (because the Christians referred to eating Christ's body and drinking His blood)
76. C
77. D
78. D
79. C
80. C
81. C
82. A
83. D

84. C
85. C
86. A (Hosanna, Word, and Sparrow are Christian music companies.)
87. B
88. C
89. D
90. B
91. D
92. C
93. D
94. C
95. D
96. B (A, C, and D are Corrie's sister, brother, and father, respectively.)
97. A
98. C (in a few cases "A" as well)
99. C
100. A
101. B
102. A
103. A
104. A
105. C
106. B
107. D
108. A

109. B
110. C

SECTION 6 (page 182)

1. D
2. A
3. A (Built in 232 in the Middle Eastern town of Dura, it's in a Yale University art museum.)
4. C
5. B
6. D
7. C
8. B
9. A
10. A
11. A
12. B
13. D
14. B
15. B
16. D
17. C
18. D
19. B
20. A
21. D
22. A

23. C
24. A (That was also the day of their annual haircut.)
25. B
26. A
27. D
28. B (It was felt that if they got used to quenching their thirst, they might quench it with wine some day.)
29. D (about 1250–1550)
30. A
31. B
32. A (Numbers 6:24)
33. D
34. B (Quakers are actually the Society of Friends; they often say they belong to "a Friends Church.")
35. A
36. A
37. C
38. A
39. D
40. D
41. D
42. A
43. A
44. B
45. A
46. B
47. D
48. C
49. D
50. C (for being traitors)
51. C
52. C
53. C (Her father ran a clock repair shop, so those terms raised no suspicion.)
54. D
55. B (The others are found in "Blest Be the Tie," "Break Thou the Bread of Life"—"my spirit pants for Thee"—and "O Worship the King"—"whose robe is the light.")
56. A
57. A
58. C
59. D (When the shepherd realized his mistake, he began worshipping Aksepsimas.)
60. C
61. D

62. A
63. B (He did, however, lean on a staff.)
64. A
65. D
66. C (The three of them formed the group Second Chapter of Acts.)
67. A
68. D
69. C
70. B (also attributed to others)
71. D
72. D (About 3,000–4,000 were sold; 1,000 drowned at sea.)
73. A
74. C
75. D
76. B
77. A (Athletes in Action)
78. A
79. B
80. D
81. A
82. D
83. A
84. B
85. C ("the birds their carols raise")
86. C
87. D (*Letters to Karen* and *Letters to Philip* are books on marriage.)
88. B
89. A
90. D
91. C
92. B
93. A
94. D
95. B
96. C
97. A
98. C
99. B
100. C
101. A (in *The Canterbury Tales*)
102. A
103. D
104. A
105. D
106. D (Regarding B, the Pilgrims believed immorality toward the Indians to be moral.)
107. A
108. B
109. D
110. C

Section 7 (page 217)

1. D (The first three are apple, milk, and salt.)
2. C
3. B
4. D
5. C
6. B (Specifically, whether the words of consecration were spoken in a low voice or sung in a loud, or "high," voice)
7. A
8. C
9. C
10. B
11. A
12. C
13. D
14. A
15. D
16. D (Of course, he may have found "A" as well.)
17. D
18. D
19. B
20. A (It now refers to non-instrumental music because instruments were thought to "cloak," or cover, the lyrics.)
21. D
22. A (A mystery play told of a Bible episode.)
23. A
24. B
25. A
26. A (This is from a second-century description.)
27. C
28. D (including the bass part)
29. C
30. B (Doctors weren't always sure how strong a dose to give in those days.)
31. A (40 percent in 1910, 60 percent in 1950, 77 percent in 1976)
32. A
33. B
34. D
35. C
36. D

37. A
38. D
39. A
40. B
41. C
42. D (Anglican churches generally offer Communion daily; Quakers don't believe in Communion.)
43. C
44. B
45. C
46. B
47. B
48. A
49. A
50. D
51. D
52. C
53. A
54. C (Ecclesiasticus is part of the Apocrypha; thus it would be found in a Catholic translation but probably not a Protestant one.)
55. A
56. A
57. D
58. A
59. B
60. C
61. C
62. D
63. D
64. C
65. B
66. D
67. B
68. D (One of the many incidents that contributed to the American prohibition against cruel and unusual punishments.)
69. A
70. A
71. B
72. A
73. D
74. B
75. A (the sonnet on his blindness)
76. D
77. C
78. A
79. D
80. C
81. D
82. A

83. D
84. D
85. C
86. A
87. D
88. C (Morality plays were allegories in which characters were given names fitting their personalities.)
89. B
90. B
91. C
92. D
93. C
94. C
95. C (In this case, guineas are British coins, not pigs.)
96. B
97. B
98. D
99. D
100. C
101. B
102. A
103. D
104. D
105. B
106. A
107. D

108. C
109. C
110. D